WORKING ON CRUISE SHIPS

A selection of other How To Books

Applying for a Job
Career Planning for Women
Doing Voluntary Work Abroad
Finding a Job in Computers
Finding a Job with a Future
Finding Work Overseas
Freelance Dee-Jaying
Getting a Job Abroad
Getting a Job in America
Getting a Job in Australia
Getting a Job in Travel & Tourism
Getting into Films & Television
Getting that Job
Getting Your First Job
How to Be a Freelance Sales Agent
How to Be a Freelance Secretary
How to Do Voluntary Work Abroad
How to Find Temporary Work Abroad
How to Get a Job in Europe
How to Get a Job in France

How to Get a Job in Germany
How to Get into Radio
How to Know Your Rights at Work
How to Market Yourself
How to Return to Work
How to Start a New Career
How to Work from Home
How to Work in an Office
How to Work in Retail
Living & Working in China
Passing that Interview
Surviving Redundancy
Working as a Holiday Rep
Working for the Environment
Working in Hotels and Catering
Working in Japan
Working in Photography
Working on Contract Worldwide
Working with Horses
Writing a CV that Works

Other titles in preparation.

The How To series now contains more than 200
titles in the following categories:

Business & Management
Computer Basics
General Reference
Jobs & Careers
Living & Working Abroad
Personal Finance
Self-Development
Small Business
Student Handbooks
Successful Writing

Please send for a free copy of the latest catalogue for full details
(see back cover for address)

JOBS & CAREERS

WORKING ON CRUISE SHIPS

How to have the time of your life working around the world

Steve Marks

STOP! – I HAVEN'T FINISHED PACKING YET!

How To Books

By the same author in this series:

Working as a Holiday Rep

Cartoons by Mike Flanagan

British Library Cataloguing in Publication Data
A catalogue record for this book is available from the British Library.
Copyright © 1996 by Steve Marks

Published by How To Books Ltd, 3 Newtec Place, Magdalen Road, Oxford, OX4
1RE, United Kingdom. Tel: (01865) 793806. Fax: (01865) 248780.
e-mail: info@howtobooks.co.uk
www.howtobooks.co.uk

First edition 1996
Second impression 1999

Note: The material contained in this book is set out in good faith for general
guidance and no liability can be accepted for loss or expense incurred as a
result of relying in particular circumstances on statements made in the book.
The laws and regulations are complex and liable to change, and readers
should check the current position with the relevant authorities before making
personal arrangements.

Cover design Shireen Nathoo Design. Cover image Photo Disc
Produced for How To Books by Deer Park Productions.
Typeset by The Baskerville Press Limited, Salisbury, Wiltshire.
Printed and bound by Cromwell Press, Trowbridge, Wiltshire.

Contents

List of Illustrations

Preface

The 1990s have proved to be the decade of the rebirth of cruising. After the demise of most of the great ocean liners in the 1960s and 70s cruising has suddenly become fashionable again.

More new cruise ships are being launched this year than any year for decades. This year also sees the debut of the world's first purpose-built 3,400 passenger cruise ship. Many new companies are starting up too: two brand new cruise lines have started up in the United Kingdom in the last two years alone.

All this means a massive demand for people to work on these new ships. It's estimated that there are now over 110,000 people working in the industry, crewing almost 200 cruise ships, in every corner of the world.

So, there are now more opportunities to work on board cruise ships than for the past 40 or 50 years. Of course, as a member of the crew on board a cruise ship, you won't be able to spend every day sunning yourself on deck or exploring foreign ports. But it is one of the few jobs where you really do get paid to travel the world.

I have written this book in response to the rebirth of the cruise industry and to many requests for good, reliable information on how to find a job on board ship. I hope you find it helpful and that, very soon, you too will be starting a new life on the ocean wave!

Good luck!

Steve Marks

IS THIS YOU?

Ship's officer

Cleaner

DJ

Ship's rating

Doctor

Chef

Carpenter

Nurse

Kitchen porter

Plumber

Shop manager

Restaurant manager

Electrician

Shop assistant

Restaurant waiter/steward

Painter

Photographer

Wine waiter

Purser

Casino croupier

Barman

Purser's assistant

Cashier

Cocktail waiter

Secretary

Tour guide

Cruise director

Office clerk

Sports instructor

Cruise department staff

Telephone operator

Beauty therapist

Entertainer

Printer

Gym instructor

Children's host/ess

Journalist

Masseur/se

Children's entertainer

Hotel manager

Hairdresser

Children's nanny

Cabin steward

(Most jobs are equally available to men and women.)

1
What You Need to Know about the Cruise Industry

A CITY AT SEA

To the passenger a cruise ship might be no more than a floating hotel. It takes them from one glamorous destination to another, feeds and entertains them lavishly, and provides them with a place to rest between exotic ports of call.

But when you join the crewing side of things you will find it is so much more than that. Quite literally a cruise ship is a city at sea. Some of the newest ships are in fact much more than that: they are massive **floating holiday resorts**, complete with every facility you could imagine.

On the one hand there are the obvious facilities like restaurants, bars, shops and hair salons. These are the 'front of house' services that the passenger uses every day and, of course, they have to be staffed. But this is very much the tip of the iceberg. Think of it this way: a cruise ship has to be totally self-contained. A ship at sea can't just stop off at the nearest bakers for breakfast rolls, or phone a shore-based electrician to fix a broken light fitting. The ship has to be self-sufficient and everything has to be done on board from baking bread to redecorating the cabins.

So there are more jobs than you might expect. In fact, a cruise ship offers very much the same range of job opportunities that you would find in any city.

You might be interested in one of the front-of-house jobs, like restaurant waiter or waitress, shop assistant or entertainer. But there are lots of opportunities behind the scenes too, doing technical work, maintenance work and the many other support services that keep the ship cruising.

So, whatever sort of work you can do, there is more than likely to be an opening for you.

WHAT SORT OF JOBS ARE AVAILABLE?

Generally, if a job exists on dry land then it will exist somewhere on a cruise ship. The title of the job might be different and it may be performed in a slightly different way but at the end of the day it is essentially the same job.

Most cruise ships divide the operations on board ship into several different departments.

The Deck Department

The job of the Deck Department is to actually sail the ship. It is responsible for journey planning, navigating, safety, communications and so on. In fact, everything connected with the day-to-day movement of the ship that is not the responsibility of the Engineering Department.

Most of the deck jobs on board a cruise ship are exactly the same as on any merchant vessel. The ship's captain is in charge of the Deck Department as well as being in overall command of the ship.

The Engineering Department

The duties of this department are, of course, engineering. But that term covers a wide range of responsibilities. Most important of all is the ship's structure and equipment – the propulsion systems (the engines) and steering, the electrical systems, the electronic systems and so on. All these are maintained by engineers with a specialist knowledge of marine engineering.

In addition there are the engineering jobs that are the same as on dry land. For example, electricians, plumbers, carpenters, painters and decorators who may be involved with, for example, repairing kitchen appliances or refurbishing the cabins.

The Purser's Department

The purser and his staff look after all the management and administration on board ship. This includes such matters as accounting, finance, personnel and providing customer services. A lot of the jobs in the Purser's Department are the same as in a hotel or an office on dry land.

The Catering Department

Food is a very important part of life at sea. The Catering Department on board a ship operates for 24 hours a day, serving both the passengers and the crew. All their food has to be bought, prepared, cooked and served so this is one of the biggest departments on board ship and employs everyone from kitchen porters to top class chefs and restaurant waiters or stewards to restaurant management.

The Hotel Department
Staff who work in the Hotel Department are responsible for the cleaning and upkeep of the cabins and public areas. So, for example, jobs in this department include cabin stewards or stewardesses and cleaners plus all the management and supervisory staff involved with keeping the ship immaculate. As with some other departments the work is very similar to that in a hotel.

The Bar Department
A large cruise ship has many different bars, from cocktail bars, poolside bars and show lounges to casino bars. All this has to be run smoothly and efficiently requiring everything from bar staff, waiters and cellar staff to management.

The Cruise Department
The Cruise Department is a front-of-house department and it is also the one that offers some of the most exciting work. The Cruise Department is charged with looking after the passengers during their cruise and making sure they have an enjoyable time. It is responsible for putting on evening shows, parties and receptions, daytime entertainments and sporting activities and so on. It employs people from dozens of different fields such as singers and dancers, children's entertainers and sports instructors.

Other Departments
By no means do all the jobs on board a cruise ship fall into the departments above. In addition, there are a number of other facilities on board which contribute to the running of the ship.

Very often these facilities are operated not by the cruise line but by outside companies who pay the cruise line for the right to operate them. Facilities operated on this basis are know as **concessions**, and the companies which operate them are known as **concessionaires**.

Concessionaires operate facilities like hair salons, retail shops, photography services, casinos and health clubs. They employ all the same people that any similar land-based service would. So far as the crew member is concerned the important thing to note is that they are employed by the concessionaire and not by the cruise line.

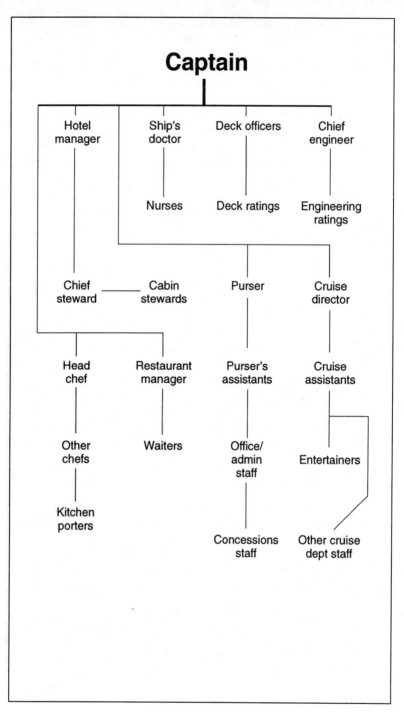

Fig.1. The ship's company.

LIVING AND WORKING AT SEA

Although many of the jobs carried out on a cruise ship are similar to those on dry land, they are carried out under quite different circumstances. For example, even when you've done a long, hard day on the ship you can't just go home, or go out on the town with your friends! Crew members on a cruise ship not only work on the ship but, of course, live with it on a 24-hour 7-days-a-week basis too.

In this section we'll look at a few of the pros and cons to help you decide whether or not this is the sort of work you would like.

Weighing up the pros and cons
It's hard work!
Working on a cruise ship can be fun but it is most definitely hard work too. You'll probably work a **longer day** than normal (ten or twelve hour shifts are common) and may have only one day a week off – perhaps not even that in some cases. Because of this it's important that you actually enjoy your job and also that you would enjoy a hectic lifestyle.

It calls for team effort
The crew of a cruise ship is very much a **team** who all work together to produce a highly polished, professional product – an enjoyable cruise. Every crew member very much relies on other people to do their job properly so that they can, in turn, do their job properly. If any member of the team doesn't fit in then chaos can result.

You won't necessarily live in luxury
Although most ships offer a luxurious standard of living for passengers this isn't the case for the crew. Crew accommodation tends to be adequate but fairly **basic** and often quite cramped. You'll be provided with everything you need but not a luxury suite with room service (unless you're the captain, of course!). Most accommodation is shared with other crew members.

Unless you are an officer or employed in the Cruise Department or one of the concessions you probably won't be able to use all the facilities that the passengers have access to.

You'll need to be flexible

Would-be crew members need to be flexible and be able to travel anywhere at **short notice.** They'll also be away from home for several months at a time. This is why the job attracts a lot of single people. If you have a partner then you'll have to accept that you won't see them for several months at a time.

The work can be irregular

Most cruise ships do not offer their crew indefinite employment but hire their staff on **short contracts** of, typically, between three and eight months. If you do your job well then you'll usually be asked back on another contract. However, it is never guaranteed: once your contract is up you may have to start the jobsearch again.

This makes a cruise ship career a rather insecure way of life in some ways.

But it is well paid

Undoubtedly cruise ship jobs are quite well paid. Plus, as everything is provided apart from personal clothing, toiletries and so on, most crew members find they can save quite a lot of money on each trip.

Having said this, many crew members are paid on a **salary plus tips** basis. That is, a small salary which is made up by tips from passengers. (On most cruise lines passengers are expected to tip by way of custom.)

And the benefits are good

Working on board ship offers an opportunity to visit some marvellous places since cruise ships tend to sail only in the nicer parts of the world such as the Mediterranean and Caribbean Seas, Alaska and so on. You'll be able to visit these places for next to nothing.

You should know, however, that you won't necessarily get time off in every port.

A YEAR IN THE LIFE OF *ORIANA*

Cruise ships sail in all the four corners of the world, with the Caribbean and Mediterranean Seas being the most popular cruising arenas. All the different cruise lines and ships operate different itineraries. However, to give you some idea of the cruises operated the following itinerary is that followed by P&O's 69,000-ton cruise ship *Oriana* in the current year.

The World Cruise

Southampton
Madeira
Barbados
St Lucia
Aruba
Panama Canal
Acapulco
San Francisco
Honolulu
Papeete, Tahiti
Auckland
Sydney
Melbourne

Fremantle
Bali
Hong Kong
Kota Kinabalu, Malaysia
Singapore
Mauritius
Durban
Cape Town
Walvis Bay, Namibia
Cape Verde Islands
Tenerife
Southampton

Caribbean Calypso Cruise

Southampton
Bermuda
St Thomas
Antigua
Grenada

Mayreau
Barbados
Vigo, Spain
Southampton

Canary Islands Spring Cruise

Southampton
Madeira
La Palma
Tenerife

Lanzarote
Vigo, Spain
Southampton

Istanbul Explorer Cruise

Southampton
Gibraltar
Nauplia, Greece
Dikili, Turkey
Istanbul

Nesbur, Bulgaria
Yalta, Ukraine
Palma, Majorca
Southampton

Baltic Treasures Cruise

Southampton
Copenhagen
St Petersburg
Helsinki
Visby, Sweden

Travemunde, Germany
Oslo
Amsterdam
Southampton

The Italian Affair Cruise

Southampton
Palma, Majorca
Cannes
Livorno, Italy

Elba, Italy
Gibraltar
Southampton

Land of the Midnight Sun Cruise

Southampton
Hardangerfjord, Norway
Andalsnes, Norway
Narvik, Norway
Ofotfjord, Norway

North Cape, Norway
Trondheim, Norway
Bergen, Norway
Southampton

Mediterranean Magic Cruise

Southampton
Gibraltar
Elba, Italy
Livorno, Italy

Alghero, Sardinia
Monte Carlo
Barcelona
Southampton

A Summer Medley

Southampton
Madeira
Tenerife
Lanzarote
Casablanca

Praia da Rocha, Portugal
Lisbon
La Coruna, Spain
Southampton

Summer Gold Cruise

Southampton
Tangier
Cannes
Elba, Italy

Naples
Sidi Bou Said, Tunisia
Vigo, Spain
Southampton

A Greek Idyll Cruise

Southampton
Gibraltar
Loutraki, Greece
Corfu

Preveza, Greece
Syracuse, Italy
Palma, Majorca
Southampton

La Dolce Vita Cruise

Southampton
Gibraltar
Livorno, Italy
Monte Carlo

Sete, France
Ibiza
Praia da Rocha, Portugal
Southampton

Taste of Africa Cruise

Southampton
Praia da Rocha, Portugal
Casablanca
Lanzarote

La Palma
Madeira
Vigo
Southampton

Aegean Explorer Cruise

Southampton
Gibraltar
Gythion, Greece
Piraeus, Greece

Kusadasi, Turkey
Palma, Majorca
Southampton

Autumn Medley Cruise

Southampton
Vigo, Spain
Sidi Bou Said, Tunisia
Naples

Ajaccio
Barcelona
Southampton

Le Party Français Cruise

Southampton
Le Havre

Cherbourg
Southampton

Mediterranean Treasures Cruise

Southampton
Gibraltar
Limassol, Cyprus
Haifa, Israel

Piraeus, Greece
Malaga
Southampton

Canaries Carousel Cruise

Southampton
Gran Canaria
Lanzarote

Tenerife
La Palma
Madeira

Caribbean Christmas Cruise

Southampton
Madeira
Antigua
Barbados

St Vincent
Martinique
Vigo, Spain
Southampton

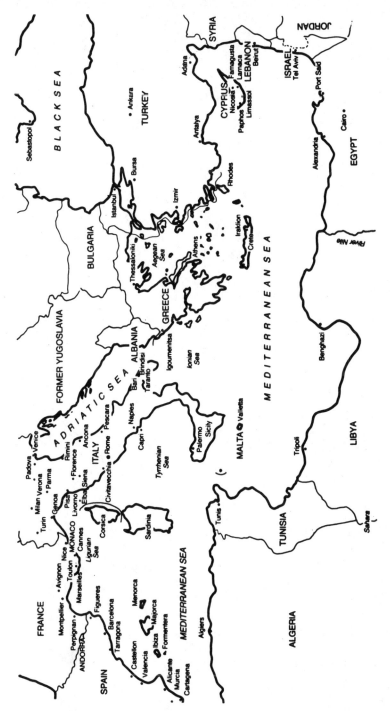

Fig.2. The Mediterranean — one of the world's main cruising arenas.

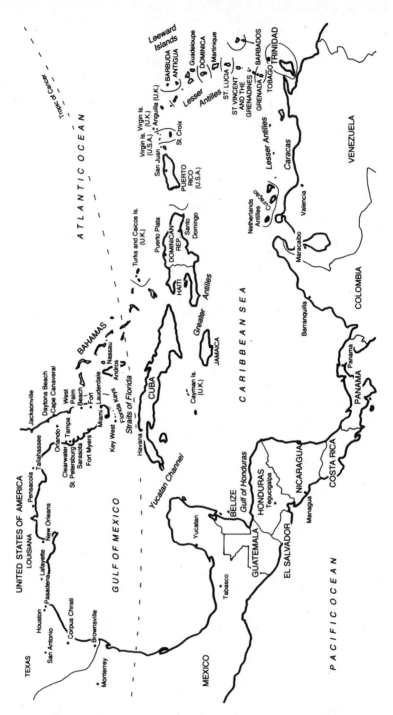

Fig.3. The Caribbean – another of the world's main cruising arenas.

WHAT SKILLS, EXPERIENCE AND QUALIFICATIONS DO YOU NEED?

It is important to be aware that, with a few exceptions, cruise ships do not employ people without any previous skills, experience and qualifications. For most jobs they prefer to recruit people who have already carried out that job on dry land.

Skills
These are the skills that you will find useful:

- being able to **get on well** with your fellow workers

- being used to **dealing with the public**

- being able to do your job to a **very high standard**

- **language skills** are not essential but very much sought after by employers. If you have a working knowledge of another major world language (such as French, German or Italian) you will find it much easier to get a job. You do not necessarily need to be qualified in it.

Qualifications
With the exception of Deck Department and Engineering Department staff there are no special qualifications which are exclusive to cruise ship crew. The qualifications which apply to jobs in, for example, the Catering Department or the Hotel Department are those which apply to similar work on dry land.

Details of qualifications which may be required for particular jobs are given under the individual job descriptions in Chapter 4.

Experience
It is very important to point out that you should have **some experience** of doing the job on dry land before you apply to work on a cruise ship. Cruise ships do not generally have the time or resources to train people on board so you must know how to carry out your job before you take up a position. For example, if you want to work in the hair salon on board a cruise ship you should have worked in a land-based hair salon first.

If you do not have the relevant experience it is advisable to obtain it in a job on dry land first and then apply to a cruise line.

You do not need to have any experience of working at sea before. It doesn't even matter if you have never been on board a ship.

WHAT PAY, CONDITIONS AND BENEFITS CAN YOU EXPECT?

Pay

It varies a great deal depending on the job and the cruise line in question but, generally, pay is comparable with or less than the pay offered for a similar job on dry land.

If you are doing a job which involves contact with the public you will normally be paid a fairly small basic wage but also receive tips from passengers or a commission on products sold. Such tips are virtually guaranteed since on most ships passengers are expected to tip by custom.

Benefits

You will also normally receive all accommodation, food, and a uniform free of charge.

If you join the ship in a country other than your home country then you will usually be given a free flight out to the ship, plus a free return flight if your contract ends when the ship is away from your home country.

Your pay will often be paid to you without any deduction for tax. However, whether you have to pay tax later on depends on the amount of time you are out of the country.

Conditions

Except for some Deck Department and Engineering Department jobs cruise ship crew are not normally recruited on indefinite contracts as with most jobs on dry land. When you take a job you will usually be offered a **fixed term contract**. This varies but it is often between three months and eight months.

Your contract is very likely to be extended but you cannot always depend on this as it, in turn, depends on how many passengers book for next season's cruises.

Some cruise lines pay a bonus to crew who undertake a second and subsequent contract. This applies to certain hard-to-fill positions.

IS THIS WORK FOR YOU?

Answer our simple self-assessment quiz to decide whether this work is really for you:

1. Do you already have some experience in a shipboard job or are you willing to get some?

                                                YES   NO

2. Do you like working with people?

                                                YES   NO

3. Do you like serving the public to a very high standard?

                                                YES   NO

4. Would you mind working long hours and not having a great deal of time off?

                                                YES   NO

5. Would you mind being away from home for long periods at a time?

                                                YES   NO

6. Would you mind a certain amount of insecurity in that you may have to leave to take up a new job at short notice and may also have to look for new contracts from time to time?

                                                YES   NO

To really enjoy working at sea you should have answered YES to the first three questions and NO to the last three questions!

2
Finding your Job

SCANNING NEWSPAPERS WITH JOBS TO OFFER

Jobs on cruise ships are advertised from time to time in the national newspapers. There are not a great many in any one paper on any one day. So, rather than buying all the papers regularly it is much better to go to the library and read them all now and again.

You can find jobs advertised in all these national newspapers:

Daily Mail	*Mail on Sunday*
Daily Express	*Sunday Express*
Daily Mirror	*Independent*
Daily Star	*Guardian*
Sun	*Times*
Daily Telegraph	*Independent on Sunday*
Sunday Telegraph	*Sunday Times*

Also try these regional newspapers:

London Evening Standard
Manchester Evening News

A very good place to find vacancies is the *Overseas Jobs Express* newspaper, available at some libraries or on subscription from: *Overseas Jobs Express,* Premier House, Shoreham Airport, Sussex BN43 5FF. Tel: (01273) 440220.

KNOWING THE MAGAZINES WITH JOBS TO OFFER

Trade and professional magazines and journals are the best types of magazines to read for this type of work. Again, vacancies are not advertised frequently so, unless you already buy the magazine, it is best to read it at your local library.

You can find jobs advertised and other job leads in all these magazines:

British Journal of Photography
Caterer and Hotelkeeper
Hair & Beauty Salon
Hair
Hairdresser's Journal International
Music Week
Retail Jeweller
Stage and Television Today
The Photographer
Travel Trade Gazette
Travel Weekly

A very good place to look for these vacancies is a newsletter called *Crews 4 Cruise News.* This is published by Harp Publications Ltd, Thames House, Swan Street, Old Isleworth, Middlesex TW7 6TW. Tel: (0181) 568 6668.

USING AN EMPLOYMENT AGENCY

There are a number of employment agencies in the UK, mainland Europe and also the USA which specialise in filling vacancies on cruise ships. These agencies are hired by the individual cruise lines to find suitable people.

It is well worth contacting all these agencies to find out if they may have a job suitable for you. No reputable agency should charge the employee, as the employer pays their fees. A list of some of the main agencies and details of the type of jobs they handle are given in Chapter 5.

Here is how to get the best results when using employment agencies.

Getting the best results

1. Make a list of which agencies handle the type of work you are looking for. (Not all agencies handle every type of work.)

2. Write a letter to each agency, telling them:
   - what **type of job** you are looking for
   - what relevant **qualifications** you have
   - what relevant **experience** you have
   - what relevant **skills** and interests you have.

3. Enclose a copy of your **up-to-date CV** (more about this in Chapter 3).

4. Enclose a good head and shoulders **photograph** of yourself.

If the agency thinks you are suitable for any of the jobs they handle they will usually interview you and, if you are successful, they will keep your name on file. When a suitable job comes along they will then contact you.

Because it may take some time for any one agency to find a suitable vacancy you should register with as many agencies as possible to increase your chances of being offered a job.

USING THE JOB CENTRE

It has to be said that not a great number of jobs on cruise ships are handled through the Employment Service Job Centres. However, this may be a route worth following, especially if you are unemployed.

Getting the best results

1. Decide what type of work you want to do. This should be something in which you have experience.

2. Make a list of the qualifications, skills and experience you thing you can offer.

3. Tell your local Job Centre that you are interested in any jobs available on cruise ships.

Your Job Centre should be able to find out if any vacancies are held on file that would suit your requirements at any Job Centre in the UK. They can also tell you about any suitable vacancies in other European Union countries. If you are interested in this ask for details of the EURES (European Employment Services) system which can provide information on vacancies in all the other EU countries, together with Norway. (The EU countries are Austria, Belgium, Denmark, Finland, France, Germany, Greece, Ireland, Italy, Luxembourg, Netherlands, Portugal, Spain, Sweden, UK.)

The EURES system is run by the Overseas Placing Unit, Level 2, Rockingham House, 123 West Street, Sheffield S1 4ER. Tel: (0114) 259 6051.

APPLYING DIRECT TO A CRUISE LINE

One of the best ways to find a suitable job is to make an application direct to a **cruise line** or to a **concessionaire** (the companies who operate such facilities as hair salons and casinos).

This method can be very successful as many cruise lines receive a large number of direct applications of this type and so rarely need to advertise their vacancies. So, it is definitely a good idea to make a direct application rather than just waiting for advertised vacancies to appear.

A list of the world's main cruise lines and concessionaires is given in Chapter 5.

Applying step-by-step

Here's how to make an application direct to a cruise line:

1. Read the description of cruise lines in Chapter 5 and decide which you think you would be suitable for. (Different cruise lines operate in different parts of the world and have a different style of service on board.)

2. Decide what type of work you want to do. This will depend on your experience and qualifications. If you wish to apply for several types of work then this is perfectly acceptable.

3. Compile a CV for yourself. (More information on this is given in Chapter 3.)

4. Mail out a copy of your CV to each cruise line together with a covering letter which introduces yourself. (More information on this is given in Chapter 3.)

5. If your job involves contact with the public then send a head and shoulders photograph with each application. A passport-type photograph is OK as long as it is clear.

Do's and Don'ts

Do apply to as many cruise lines as you like.

Don't apply to just one as it may take some time for a suitable job to become available. One good way of doing this is to apply to three or four companies each week until the right job offer comes along.

Don't just apply to the cruise lines in your own country. The UK is home to about only ten per cent of the world's cruise ship fleet. Most of the work's cruise lines have an operating base in Florida in the USA and some of the largest fleets are owned by Dutch, Italian, Greek and Norwegian companies. Since most of these recruit English-speaking staff you can also apply direct to them.

FINDING A JOB BY WORD OF MOUTH

As with any other type of work, not all jobs on cruise ships are found by conventional means such as answering advertisements and writing letters. Some of them are obtained by what we might call networking or 'word of mouth' methods.

This is not a method of finding a job you can completely rely on. However, it is worth trying to find out about jobs by these word of mouth methods.

Using your initiative

- If you know anyone who works on a cruise ship, any other merchant ship, or at a port ask them if they know of any contacts.

- If you know anyone who has ever worked on a cruise ship, any other ship, or at a port then ask them for ideas.

- If you are interested in jobs in the Hotel, Catering or Bar Departments or the concessions then ask around at your local large hotels, restaurants, nightclubs, gyms, sports centres, hair salons and so on. Hotel managers, salon owners and the like often know where cruise ship vacancies can be found.

- Call the port office or harbourmaster's office in ports where cruise ships call. They may well be willing to give you tips and further leads. This applies to any cruise ship port, but the main ones in the UK are Southampton, Tilbury and Dover.

- It is possible to make a telephone call to ships using the Inmarsat satellite system and so you could call them up and ask if they have any vacancies. Telephone numbers for ships which are equipped with this facility can be obtained by dialling 153 in the UK. However, do note that the cost of making an Inmarsat call is high.

3
Applying for your Job

KNOWING WHAT EMPLOYERS WANT

When first applying for any new job it is always a good idea to think careful about exactly what the employer is looking for before taking your application any further. This has two benefits: first, it will help you decide if the job is really for you and, secondly, it will help you decide how to put over your own personal skills and qualities to best effect.

In this section we will go through some of the things that cruise ship employers are looking for.

Experience
As we have already said you should already have some land-based experience in your job. But employers really like people who can show a **broad range** of experience. For example, if your job involves contact with the public then experience of serving the public in several ways will be an advantage.

High standards of service
All functions on board cruise ships are carried out to a high standard. So it is important that you can carry out your work to a high standard. For example, service in the Hotel, Catering and Bar Departments is usually similar to that in a four or five star hotel.

Professionalism
It is important to be professional about your work. That is, you need not only to be skilled in it but also to **take a pride in your work** and in achieving excellent results every time. This is not always easy when you are working long hours in a fast-moving environment.

Reliability

Most employers will want to satisfy themselves that you will stay for the full duration of your contract. Obviously, once you have joined a ship you cannot easily be replaced in a foreign port. So, you must give the clear impression that this type of work is what you do.

Interviewers are very wary of recruiting new crew members whom they suspect might 'jump ship' in an exotic foreign port when the novelty wears off. Also, you will stand a much better chance of being offered the job if you give the truthful impression that you want to make a long-term career out of working on board ship and aren't just going to 'give it a go'.

High standards of presentation

It is very important that you are immaculately turned out when you work on board ship. This applies particularly to crew who have contact with the passengers but also to behind-the-scenes crew too, to a lesser extent. Again, if you consider that many cruise ships operate to the same standards of service as a top-class international hotel then you will get an idea of the sort of people the employer is looking for.

Enthusiasm

You really do need to show that you are **hard working** and **energetic**. Shifts on board ship can be much longer than on dry land. In particular, you certainly wouldn't want to give the impression that you are a nine-to-five type person.

A cheerful personality

You may find this a strange quality for a cruise ship employer to place much importance on, but they do. Obviously, working in the confines of a ship – and living on board too – can be quite stressful and demanding. But since many of the passengers will have paid several thousands of pounds for their cruise, it is very important that the crew are pleasant and professional with them. It is equally important that you are fairly cheerful and easy going off-duty so that you can do your job professionally when you are on duty.

We will say a little more about interview technique later in this chapter. However, if you can bear in mind what the employer is looking for at all stages of your application then you will be doing a great deal to boost your chances of being offered a job.

MAKING THE BEST OF YOUR SKILLS AND EXPERIENCE

As with any other type of work it is usually the case that cruise ship jobs go to the best applicants who not only are the best, but who look the best. It doesn't matter how good you think you are at your job. If you can't put this over well then you will be at a disadvantage when it comes to selection.

There are, therefore, quite a few things you can do to make the very best of your skills and experience. So, don't leave these to chance: go through these points and see what you could do before you even make your application.

Ensuring that your achievements are recognised

Often it does not matter how good you are a a particular job but how your achievement is **recognised** and **recorded**. In other words, it is often those who have the qualifications, rather than those who can perform the task, who get the job.

Therefore it is a good idea to look at your area of work and see how you can improve your qualifications in this area. Are there any courses or exams you can take? For example, are there further NVQs (National Vocational Qualifications) or SVQs (Scottish Vocational Qualifications) you could take? Or are there further professional qualifications you could obtain: for example, a Basic Food Hygiene Certificate (for catering staff)?

Ensuring you have all your certificates

This point should be read in conjunction with the previous section. If you have any relevant qualifications then make sure you have the certificates to prove it. If they have been lost obtain certified copies.

At this point it should be said that British qualifications are not always officially recognised in foreign countries. So, if you want to apply for a job abroad, it is a good idea to obtain a prospectus for the course of study you have followed. Then, when· you attend an interview, you will be able to show the employer exactly what skills your qualifications refer to.

Obtaining as many references as possible

Because of the high standards involved in this type of work, references are always useful as they show the employer that you can actually do the job, not just that you have a certificate that says you can. So it is a very good idea to obtain as many written references as you can before making your first application.

The very best references come from past (or even present) employers. These can be full or part-time employers. Academic references, from your school or college, are next best. References from family or friends can be useful, although they do not carry as much weight as either employer or academic references.

It is a good idea to contact people you know and ask them if they would be willing to write you a short reference. Alternatively, ask them if they would allow you to give their name and address to a future employer if they ask for a reference.

Collecting evidence of interests and hobbies

Every job applicant can produce certificates and evidence of their experience. However, what makes a good applicant stand out is any interests or hobbies they have which are unique to them.

So think about your interests and hobbies. Make a list of these for use in your application.

Always having a proper CV

This is probably the most effective way to make the most of your skills and experience. A CV or **curriculum vitae** is a standard statement of your educational and career history and other particulars which is understood by every employer in all the main countries of the world. A good CV can be your passport into the job you really want.

You can compile your own CV or use a CV writing service to do this for you if you wish. If you want to compile your own CV then this is covered later in this chapter.

WRITING A GREAT APPLICATION LETTER

Quite often when applying for your cruise ship job you will need to write a formal application letter. This applies whether you are writing in response to an advertised vacancy, or whether you are making a speculative approach to an employer.

The application letter is your 'foot in the door' to an interview. Even if you send a CV, and even if an application form is to be completed, this letter can make all the difference. It gives the personnel officer an extra reason for reading you CV and application form.

Tips for writing an outstanding application letter

- Always start with an opening paragraph that states **what job you are applying for** (if the job is advertised) or what sort of work you are looking for (if it is a speculative application).

- In the second paragraph give **brief personal details**, such as your age and details of your background.

- In the next paragraph say **what job you are doing now** and what level you have reached in it. If your current job is not directly relevant to the job you are applying for, then explain why you want to change. If you have done a job in the past that is directly relevant then say so.

- Always say a few words about your **experience.**

- Say **why you are qualified** to do this job. Refer to any special qualifications. If you are not qualified 'on paper' then refer to any experience which you think qualifies you to do this job.

- Say why you think you are **suitable for a job on board a cruise ship** and give your main reason for wanting this job.

- Do **not** say that you would like the job for the opportunity to travel. This does not always go down well with employers. A much better reason for wanting the job is, for example, that you want to **further your career** and that you see this as a very good way of achieving that aim.

- Always offer to **attend for interview** (assuming, of course, you are willing to).

- You can either type, wordprocess or handwrite your application letter. Whichever method you use if must be **clear** and very **well presented.** Use blue or black ink on white, unlined A4 paper.

- If possible use no more than one or two sheets of paper. **One** is best if at all possible.

It is well worth taking time to write the best application letter you can. Once you have prepared a really good letter there is no reason why you cannot use it over and over again when applying to different employers. Figures 4 and 5 give two sample application letters for you to look at.

Miss Victoria Oriana   Daniel Anderson
Atlantic Cruise Lines   10 Canberra Road
PO Box 5000   London EC501AB
Southampton SO1 1AB   Tel. 0000 000 0000

                                             1 December 19xx

Dear Miss Oriana

I should like to apply for the position of Restaurant Steward with Atlantic
Cruise Lines as advertised in 'Overseas Jobs Express', 30 November.

I am 22 years old and have worked in the hotel and catering industry since
leaving school when I commenced my training as a commis waiter with
the L'Escargot Restaurant in London WC1. At the moment I am
employed as a waiter in the Ports of Call Restaurant, which is the main
restaurant within the George VI hotel here in London.

I am fully experienced in all aspects of a restaurant waiting including
silver service and flambé dishes. I have also obtained NVQs at Levels 1
and 2 in Serving Food and Drink.

I would very much like to obtain a position on board a cruise ship as I feel
that it would be a job which would use my skills and experience to date to
the full. I appreciate the very high standards of service that operate on
board your ships and feel confident that I would be able to meet these
standards and also integrate well with the restaurant team.

I enclose my CV for your consideration and would be very pleased to
attend for interview if required.

Yours sincerely

Daniel Anderson

Fig.4. Applying for an advertised job.

The Personnel Department   Daniel Anderson
East Coast Cruise Lines   10 Canberra Road
PO Box 5000   London EC50 1AB
Miami FL33132 USA   Tel. 0000 000 0000

                                              1 December 19xx

Dear Sirs

I am writing to ask if you currently have any vacancies for the position of Restaurant Steward.

I am 22 years old and have worked in the hotel and catering industry since leaving school when I commenced my training as a commis waiter with the L'Escargot Restaurant in London WC1. At the moment I am employed as a waiter in the Ports of Call Restaurant, which is the main restaurant within the George VI hotel here in London.

I am fully experienced in all aspects of a restaurant waiting including silver service and flambé dishes. I have also obtained NVQs at Levels 1 and 2 Serving Food and Drink.

I would very much like to obtain a position on board a cruise ship as I feel that it would be a job which would use my skills and experience to date to the full. I appreciate the very high standards of service that operate on board your ships and feel confident that I would be able to meet these standards and also integrate well with the restaurant team.

I enclose my CV for your consideration and would be very pleased to hear if you have any vacancies for which I might be suitable.

Yours faithfully

Daniel Anderson

Fig. 5. Making a speculative application.

COMPILING A PROFESSIONAL CV

The CV or **curriculum vitae** is one of the most important documents in your job application. For a start, it provides all the relevant information about you on one simple sheet of paper: the employer doesn't have to go wading through a letter to extract what they really need to know. Secondly, a well prepared CV is evidence of the fact that you can work professionally and to a high standard, both of which are very important qualities for this type of work.

If you don't have a CV at present it is a very good idea to compile one now. It will then be ready and waiting to send off with your applications. If you do have a CV then review it before every application to make sure it is as up to date as possible.

Key pointers to use

Here are some pointers that will make your CV stand out:

- Always head the page with **CURRICULUM VITAE**. This is a simple point which is often overlooked but it helps to draw the reader's eye straight to the document.

- Always include **your full name**. Put your first name first, followed by any middle names and your surname.

- Always give a **full postal address**. State the country if you are making an application to a foreign country.

- Always give a **telephone number**, with both day and evening numbers if possible. Often interviews are given to people who can be called in at short notice.

- Next put your **educational history**. Younger applicants should detail all schools attended. Older applicants normally just refer to their secondary education. State all qualifications obtained.

- The next section should cover your **work history**. Start with your current job and work back through at least your last three or four jobs (if applicable).

- It is a very good idea to state your **main responsibilities** in each job and also, if space allows, your main reason for leaving.

- Mention any **vocational qualifications** you have separately from your school qualifications since it is important that these stand out.

- Always say a few words about **hobbies and interests** as, again, this will help you stand out from the crowd.

- If you have any special **language abilities** then always include this in a separate section. Also state your level of competence, *eg* beginner, intermediate, advanced.

- Your CV must always be **typed** or **wordprocessed**. Handwritten CVs are not acceptable. If you don't have the use of a typewriter or wordprocessor then pay a typing service to do this for you and have some copies made. Photocopies are acceptable so long as they are of very good quality.

- Your CV should fit onto **one side** of one sheet of A4 paper. If it really has to be longer then it can be but only if you are sure you cannot make it any shorter.

- If your job involves working with the public then enclose a passport-sized **photograph**.

Figure 6 is a good example of how to set a CV out. Figure 7 shows a blank CV form which gives the relevant translations for a CV in, respectively, English, French, German, Spanish and Italian.

CURRICULUM VITAE

Alison Jane Green

Home Address:
2 Queen Elizabeth Way
Cunardsville
CU1 1AB
United Kingdom

Tel: 0000 000000 (day) 0000 000000 (eve)

Date of birth: 1 January 1970

Education:

1981 – 1986: City High School, Cundardsville. I followed a course of study leading to O-level qualifications in the following subjects: Mathematics (grade C), English (grade C), Chemistry (grade C), History (grade B).

1975 – 1981: The Grange Primary School, Cunardsville.

Career:

1990 – present: Manageress, ABC Duty Free, Cunardsville Airport. I am responsible for the management of the perfume and cosmetics counters within the duty free shop. This includes overall responsibility for personnel, display, accounting and for meeting sales targets.

1987 – 1990: Sales Assistant, Smith's Department Store, Cunardsville. My position involved training in all aspects of the retail of perfumes and cosmetics including display, demonstration and sales techniques. Reason for leaving: to take a position involving more responsibility.

Other qualifications: Dipolma in Sales Promotion and Selling.
Hobbies and interests: Swimming, listening to music.
Languages: I speak a little conversational French and Italian.

Fig.6. A sample CV.

CURRICULUM VITAE

Name/Nom/Name/Appellidos/Nome:

Address/Adresse/Anschrift/Dirección/Indirizzo:

Tel:

Date of birth/Date de naissance/Geburtsdatum/Fecha de nacimiento/Data di nascita:

Nationality/Nationalité/Staatsangehörigkeit/Nacionalidad/Cittadinanza:

Education/Etudes/Ausbildungagang/Estudios/Studi:

Work experience/Expérience professionelle/Berufserfahrung/Experiencia profesional/Esperienza professionale:

Fig.7. A model CV for Europe.

References/Référence/Referenz/Referencia/Referenza (Attestato)

1.	2.

Interests outside work/Activités extra-professionelles/
Ausserberufliche/Actividades extra-profesionales/Attività o attitudini
extraprofessionali:

Other information/Information supplémentaire/Zusätzlich
information/Información adicional/Informazioni supplementare:

Date/Date/Datum/Fecha/Date:

FILLING IN AN APPLICATION FORM

You won't always be asked to fill in an application form for this type of work. Often you will be asked just to send in a letter or a CV. However, if you are supplied with a form then it is well worth while taking plenty of time to complete it properly. A lot of application forms are completed wrongly and so are discarded without even being read. If you complete your form properly then you will already have a head start over the many other applicants.

Five key tips
Here are some tips on how to complete the form:

- Take a **photocopy** of the form first and complete that. Then check it over. When you are satisfied that all the answers are correct and read well then copy them over to the original form.

- **Read the instructions** on the form carefully and follow them exactly. If it says write in block capitals, or in black ink, then do so. (This is often so that the form can be photocopied and distributed to several people. If you write in blue ink, for example, it may not photocopy well.)

- Even if you have given some of the information in a covering letter or CV repeat it on the form if asked for. Do **not** put 'refer to my CV' or whatever as the person reading the CV may not bother.

- Give **full and complete answers**. If you really need to say more than there is pace for on the form then attach another sheet and refer to it on the application form. Only do this if you have to and keep the attached sheets to a minimum, but it is better than giving an incomplete answer.

- If there is a question which asks 'Please state why you want this job and what you think you could offer this company' then do think about your answer **very carefully**. Plan an answer that is concise but gives the reader really solid reasons for wanting to take your application further, especially points which other people are unlikely to have mentioned.

Do's and Don'ts

Don't say that you would like to travel.

Don't say that you think you would find the work exciting.

Don't say you are bored with your present job. (The reader will tend to assume you will also get bored with this job.)

Do say that you want to further your career.

Do say that you think you would enjoy the challenge.

Do refer to your experience.

Figure 8 shows a sample application form. You might like to photocopy this form and practise answering the questions. Once you have the answers on paper you can then use them in just about any application form you need to complete in the future!

OCEAN CRUISE AGENCIES LIMITED

Application for Employment

- Please complete every section of this form using a black ballpoint pen. If there is insufficient space to give a complete answer then please attach a separate sheet.

Position applied for:

PERSONAL DETAILS

Surname:
Forenames:
Marital status: Single/Engaged/Married/Divorced/Separated/
Widowed
Date of birth:
Age:
Place of birth:
Nationality:
Address:
Telephone (include area code):
Address of parents or
guardian (if different):

Please give any dates in the near future when you will not be available for interview:

Where did you hear of this vacancy?:

UNIFORM DETAILS

Female
UK size:
Bust:
Waist:
Hips:
Height:

Fig. 8. A sample application form.

Male
Chest:
Waist:
Inside leg:
Collar:
Height:

EMPLOYMENT HISTORY

Are you employed at present? YES/NO

If yes, please state your current employer's name, address, telephone and type of business:

Reason for wishing to leave?:

Have you previously worked in a position which involved dealing with the public and providing them with a service? YES/NO

If yes, please state your employer, name, address, telephone, type of business and your reason for leaving:

Job 1:

Job 2:

REFERENCES

Please give two employment references:

1.

2.

May we contact the above individuals/companies after interview?
YES/NO

Have you worked for our company before? YES/NO

If yes, please state position and reason for leaving:

LANGUAGE ABILITY

Do you speak any foreign languages? YES/NO

If yes, please state:

Language: Where learnt: Level of proficiency: Qualifications:

QUALIFICATIONS

Do you have any qualifications which are directly related to the job you are applying for? YES/NO

If yes, please state:

Subject: Qualification: Grade: Issuing body:

Please list any other qualifications below (*eg* GCSEs, A levels, degrees):

Subject: Qualification: Grade: Issuing body:

MEDICAL

Please give details of any illnesses you have suffered within the last 5 years and any current medical conditions:

Please state below your main reasons for applying for this job and what you think you could offer to our company:

I declare that the information on this application is correct. If employment is offered to me, it will be conditional on the receipt of satisfactory references.

Signature: Date:

- When completed please return this form to the PERSONNEL DEPARTMENT and attach 2 passport - sized photographs to the top right hand corner.

FOR PERSONNEL DEPARTMENT USE ONLY:

Fig.8. A sample application form.

PREPARING FOR YOUR INTERVIEW

If you have handled your CV, letter and application form well then you will have increased your chances of being asked for interview. Once this happens there is a great deal you can do to increase your chances of being successful.

Tips for a successful interview

- First, find out **where the interview is** and how long it is going to take you to get there. (If the company you have applied to is abroad, don't worry, they will usually arrange interviews in this country.)

- Always take **copies** of your letter, CV and application form. You can then re-read these just before the interview to make sure that everything you say agrees exactly with what you have written.

- If you haven't been asked for a **CV** so far then take some copies of this so you can hand them out at interview. It will impress!

- Decide **what you are going to wear** well before the interview. If you are hoping to get a job that involves working with the public then pay special attention to this. The interviewer will assume that the way you dress at interview is the way you would like to dress at work.

  Don't be **too casual**. Don't wear jeans and T-shirts. The b e s t things to wear are a suit (or at least a shirt and tie) for men, and a skirt and blouse, perhaps with a jacket, for women. Make sure your hair is neat and, for men, it should be above collar length. Don't wear large amounts of jewellery.

  If you are travelling some distance take some toiletries with you so that you can freshen up just before you get to the interview.

- Find out **how many people** will be conducting the interview so you won't be unduly surprised by a panel interview (of three or more people). You can phone up if you want to check on this.

- Find out if you might be asked to do any **tests** or **assessments** at the interviews. For example, some employers might ask you to write an essay or take multiple choice aptitude test. Be prepared!

- Depending on the type of work you might be asked to do a **demonstration**. For example, a beautician may be asked to perform a manicure, or a waiter could be asked to set a table. If you are applying for a job as a singer or dancer you will almost certainly be asked to sing or dance – so be prepared. You may be asked to do a set piece or something of your own. Have something prepared just in case.

- Try a **mock interview** with a friend acting as interviewer. Try the likely interview questions given later in this section!

- It is well worth going for a few interviews for jobs you are not especially interested in, just to develop your skills. You'll often find that when the pressure to succeed is off you handle the interview much better and will be able to pick up many tips you can use at a 'proper' interview.

HANDLING YOUR INTERVIEW

Of course, although preparation is important, it is what actually happens at the interview that will ascertain whether you get the job or not. So, it is a good idea to do what you can to help the interview go your way: don't sit there and let the interviewer do all the work. Make sure that you create opportunities to say what you want to say.

Improving your technique
Here are some of the ways you can improve your interview handling technique:

- Always make sure you are **on time**. Try to get there about ten minutes before the interview starts.

- **Don't smoke**, even if the interviewer says he or she doesn't mind. You won't be allowed to smoke whilst on duty and some cruise lines have no-smoking policy for crew anyway.

- Always **greet the interviewer** with a 'good morning' or 'good afternoon' and shake their hand if offered.

- Always **sit confidently**. Don't slouch in the chair.

- If it is a panel interview answer back to the person who asks the question but occasionally make eye contact with the other people on the panel too.

- When you are asked a question **never** answer just 'yes' or 'no'. Fill in with a few background details too.

- If you aren't sure what the interviewer is asking then ask them to explain the question. This is also a good technique to use if you need a little time to think of a good answer to the question.

- **Don't** criticise your present employer.

- Try to keep your answers **fairly short**, as long as you answer the question fully. If the interviewer looks bored, looks away, yawns *etc* then take it as a hint. Shut up and wait for the next question!

- **Say what you mean** rather than what you think the interviewer wants to hear. If you answer honestly then, even if you give a less-than-ideal answer, at least you will come across as an honest person, which is a very important quality for this type of work.

- Always **thank** the interviewer afterwards.

PREPARING FOR INTERVIEW QUESTIONS

Twelve likely questions

Here are some questions you could be asked at interview and some tips on how to handle them. Of course, you wouldn't say anything that was untrue but there is a lot you can do to answer the questions in a way in which the interviewer would like you to handle them.

Q. What does your present job involve?
   Give a brief run down of what you do. A 'day in the life of' report is an easy way to do this.

Q. What responsibilities do you have in your present job?
   Be sure to stress things that you are responsible for, especially things that are directly related to customer service.

Q. Would you like to tell us about yourself?
The important thing here is to be brief. Just mention your education and jobs you've done and a couple of sentences about your background.

Q. Why do you want this job?
You must always be ready for this question. We've already given you some ideas in the section on filling in application forms, so be sure to have an answer ready.

Q. Do you know much about our company?
At all costs, avoid having to say no. Try and find out a little bit about it beforehand so you can give a few basic details. If you go down to your local travel agent before the interview then you should be able to pick up that company's cruise brochures which will give you some ideas about their style of service, type of cruises operated, and also their ships.

Q. Why do you want to work for us?
This question is quite different from 'why do you want this job?' You should say why you have chosen this particular cruise line. A good tip here is to try to find out about something they are known for. For example, Carnival Cruise Lines is famous for its party cruising; Windstar, on the other hand, operates sail cruise ships.

Q. What do you see yourself doing in five years' time?
The best kind of answer to give here is to say that you hope to be in the same line of work, but in a more senior position.

Q. Have you ever been on a cruise ship before?
If you haven't then, of course, you will have to say so. Don't be afraid to say this as it doesn't really matter.
However, you must say that you have thought about the way of life which will be involved and feel sure you would like it.

Q. How do you think you would adapt to life at sea?
Always make it clear that you realise that there are disadvantages (such as limited free time, fairly cramped living and working conditions and so on) but have thought about these and are sure you could cope with them.

Q. What do you most enjoy about your work?

You could give many possible answers to this question. However, for a job that involves passenger contact, you should try to highlight a liking for serving the customer to the highest possible standard.

Q. What does your husband/wife/boyfriend/girlfriend think about you working on a ship?

It's best to say that you know that being apart for so long can be a problem – don't say that it doesn't matter as the interviewer will probably have worked at sea themselves at some time and know for a fact that it does. You should say that you have discussed it and both of you understand the problems and are prepared for the situation.

Q. What if ...?

You're very likely to be asked a 'what if' question. Such as, what would you do about a complaint, or in the case of an emergency at sea.

It's very difficult to give a proper answer to this sort of question which is, of course, why it is asked. Just try to think of a sensible, considered answer and say that you would deal with it to the best of your ability.

Nine questions you could ask

It's very important that you should ask some questions of your own at interview. This will help to show you are keen and interested. Also, quite apart from this reason, the interviewer will probably ask if you have any questions and it will give a better impression if you have some questions ready.

Here are some questions you might like to ask:

Q. What exactly would my job involve?

There is nothing wrong with asking this question so that you know exactly what will be expected of you. Different cruise lines do things in different ways. In particular many jobs on ships involve wider-ranging responsibilities than on dry land.

Q. What sort of line is Ocean Sea Cruises?

This is important because different lines have different styles of service. Some, for example, promote a family atmosphere, whereas others aim their cruises at older travellers.

Q. What ship would I be working on?

Again this question is good because it shows an interest. If you know something about that ship you will be able to demonstrate your interest by briefly discussing it.

Q. How long does the contract last?

This is quite important. It demonstrates that you know that it is normally for a fixed period only.

Q. What is the pay?

There is nothing wrong with asking this question. It shows that you are realistic. There is no set level of pay for most cruise ship jobs and you may find considerable variations from company to company.

If you are in the fortunate position of being offered more than one job you can use the employers' answers to the last two questions in order to make a decision between them.

Q. Are there opportunities to get promoted?

This is a very good question to ask since the cruise lines generally prefer people who see a future with the same cruise line.

Q. Could I contribute my ideas to the operation?

This is a good idea if you are working in a job where there is room for input of this kind, such as the hair and beauty salon, or on the entertainment side. Again, it will show your interest.

Q. What sort of people would I be working with?

This question shows that you realise the importance of teamwork on board the ship.

Q. I've heard that Ocean Sea Cruises are introducing a new cruise ship next season. Is it true?

As we have already said, try to find out what you can about the line and ask some relevant questions. (You won't necessarily be able to ask this particular question, of course.) This shows that you are interested and it also shows that you have done your homework.

INCREASING YOUR CHANCES OF GETTING THE JOB

In this chapter we've passed on lots of hints, tips and ideas that will help you make a good application. However, here are a few more tips that should increase your chances of success. Remember that, nowadays, most vacancies are oversubscribed – often several hundreds of times over – so anything you can do to make your application stand out is bound to increase your chances of success.

Tips to help you on your way

- First, check and double-check the **employer's requirements** to make sure you have them. If you don't then think twice about applying: it may be better to look for a more suitable vacancy.

- In particular, make sure you have the **necessary experience** before applying. If you don't then find out how you could get it. For example, could you get a part-time or holiday job that would give you some more relevant experience and so increase your chances of getting the job?

- If there is a phone number to call for an informal chat before you make an application then **take advantage** of this offer. This is a very good way of getting your name remembered and 'putting a face to a name' when the personnel officer comes to read the applications.

- **Telephone** to see if your application has been received, a few days after it has been delivered. Apart from serving as a double-check this will help to get your name remembered.

- Send your application in a **C4 sized envelope**, so that it does not need to be folded. This will ensure it is received in tip-top condition and immediately give a better impression.

- After the interview write a **short note of thanks**. Again, this is a very good way of trying to make sure that you stand out above the many other applicants.

- If you have **not** been successful then write or phone and ask why you have not been successful. It may take some nerve, and not all companies will tell you, but if they do this could help you to improve your next application.

- If you have not been successful ask if your application could be **kept on file** for any future vacancies. If you were suitable for the job but there were just too many successful applicants this may very often be possible. (It is also a good way of finding out if your application was up to scratch or not.)

- If this application didn't succeed **do things differently** next time. Revise your CV and application form and compose different answers to the likely interview questions. This way you can use a process of elimination to find out what methods of your own work best.

UNDERSTANDING YOUR CONTRACT OF EMPLOYMENT

What it means and what to check

Once you have been offered and have accepted a job you will normally be provided with a contract of employment. Read this carefully and make sure you understand it before signing and returning the document. Apart from being a legal contract it will also explain exactly what your **rights** and **responsibilities** are and so help you understand precisely what the job involves.

Here are some of the points you should check in your contract:

Who your employer is

It is important to check whether your employer is the cruise line itself, a concessionaire or an employment agency. You will then know who will be your immediate superior, who to direct any problems or queries to and, quite importantly, who will be paying you. If, for example, you are employed by a concessionaire your immediate superior will be the manager of the concession and not the captain of the ship. Your salary will be paid by the concessionaire rather than the cruise line.

The length of the contract

This is a very important point to check. Although it might be extended you should assume that you will have to look for another vacancy at the end of the contract period.

Your contract will most likely be for a fixed period of days or months, or it could be for the duration of a particular cruise.

Your rate of pay

Check what the rate of pay is and whether you will be paid hourly, weekly or monthly. For most jobs a monthly rate of pay is offered. Often there are no set hours. You are expected to work as and when required to complete your duties.

Also confirm when your salary will be paid. Some employers pay their crew by way of a monthly wage plus an end-of-contract bonus. The main reason for this is to discourage you from leaving part-way through your contract.

Your responsibilities

While you are checking the contract it is as well to confirm what your responsibilities will be. Exactly what is your job? To whom are you responsible? Are you responsible for any other member of the crew?

You may find that, although you are employed primarily for one job, you may be expected to do others as well. For example, an entertainer on board a cruise ship may be hired to perform a particular act but they may also be expected to act as a host or hostess to the passengers in addition.

Is there a probationary period?

Some contracts are issued subject to you performing satisfactorily during a trial period, for example 28 days. Check if such a clause applies as, if things go wrong, you could be coming home sooner than you expect!

Some contracts allow you to end the contract early if you do not settle in. However, others do not permit this and if you want to leave early you will be subject to some sort of financial penalty. For example, your air ticket home may be withdrawn.

OBTAINING PASSPORTS, VISAS AND WORK PERMITS

Applying for passports

Before applying for your first job on a cruise ship you should apply for a **full passport**, if you do not already have one. This way, if you are offered a job at short notice, you will be able to accept it and will not have to waste time waiting for a new application to be processed.

Obtaining work permits

Usually, your employer will obtain any **work permits** that are required. In many cases, however, because you are working in international waters you will require neither a work permit nor a residence permit for any particular country.

Checking visas

If you are travelling through a foreign country in order to join a ship at a foreign port you may require a **visa** to enter that country even if you do not intend staying there. For example, if you are flying to Miami to join a ship you will not require a US work permit but you may need a US visa.

As soon as you know what your route will be check with the relevant embassy to find out if any visas are required and apply well in advance.

EU citizens travelling to another EU country to work do not need a visa. The EU countries are Austria, Belgium, Denmark, Finland, France, Germany, Greece, Ireland, Italy, Luxembourg, Netherlands, Portugal, Spain, Sweden and the UK.

Job-hunting trips abroad

If you want to travel to another country in order to **look** for a job, rather than to take up a pre-arranged appointment, then you should know that the arrangements for work permits and visas may be different:

- EU citizens travelling to another EU country do not need any sort of work permit or visa.

- If travelling to any other country you may require a work permit and a visa if you intend to work, even though these may not be required for a tourist stay. Check with the relevant embassy before leaving.

- Most countries do not allow you to travel to a country and take up a job. You must first travel there, find the job, and then travel home to obtain the visa.

- If you are travelling to the USA to take up a cruise ship job you will normally require a C class (transit) or D class (seaman's) visa.

TEN TIPS TO HELP YOU SETTLE IN

Once you've joined your new ship then you're very much home and dry! However, do be prepared for something of a culture shock when you begin working and living in a totally new environment. Fortunately, there's a lot you can do to help yourself settle in. Here are some tips:

1. **Seasickness** is rarely a problem as modern cruise ships are very well stabilised and, in addition, their captains go to great lengths to avoid bad weather. If you know you are prone to seasickness – or think you might be – then you could try either pills (such as Dramamine) or patches (such as Transderm-Scop) as a remedy. Usually seasickness passes in a very short time and, in any case, your new employer will usually make allowances.

2. If you are joining a ship with a large number of foreign crew then try to learn a little of their **language** before you go, even if they speak English. (There are a lot of Dutch, Norwegian, Italian, Greek and Asian crew members on many ships.)

3. Take some **home comforts** with you, *eg* posters, books, tapes and so on.

4. If there's a choice of crew accommodation (which there often is) try to **share** with someone who does the same job. (Most accommodation is shared, apart from senior positions.)

5. Ask for any **help** you need. People are generally very friendly.

6. **Get to know** the people who have been with the ship the longest. They are a mine of useful information both about the ship and also what to see and do in port.

7. **Don't lose touch** with home. Ask friends and family to keep in touch with you. Most ships have a good mail service and mail can be dropped off and collected at the next port. Most ships are connected into the international phone network when the vessel is in port.

8.   Get involved with **onboard activities**. There are often clubs, societies and special interest groups for the crew.

9.   Go to as many **parties** as you like! There are usually cabin parties or beach parties every day, mostly with an open invitation to all crew members.

10. If you can use the ship's **facilities** and mingle with the passengers then don't hesitate.

      All officers are allowed the run of the ship. Other staff in the Deck, Engineering, Hotel, Catering and Bar Departments are not usually allowed to have the run of the ship but have their own facilities instead. Those involved in entertainment, casinos, salons, sports staff and so on, of whatever rank, are usually allowed full run of the ship.

GETTING A JOB ON A FERRY

Taking a job on a **passenger ferry** is something you might want to consider as a short-term alternative to a cruise ship. There are three reasons way this can be worth considering:

- It is often easier to get these jobs.
- They do not involve being away for as long as a contract on a cruise ship and so can act as a 'taster' of life at sea.
- Since many of the jobs are very similar, if not identical, they can provide you with the experience you need to secure a job on a cruise ship in the future.

A large number of ferry services operate in and around the UK. These include short cross-channel 'hops' such as Dover – Calais and longer trips such as to Spain, Ireland, the Netherlands and Scandinavia. Many of today's ferries are actually much more like cruise ships than ferries and, though not quite as luxurious as cruise ships, have most of the same facilities such as restaurants, bars, lounges, entertainments, cinemas and sports and leisure facilities.

Types of jobs available

Deck and Engineering Department jobs are very much the same as on cruise ships. See Chapters 1 and 4 for more details.

Opportunities in other departments vary. Only the ferries operating longer routes have a Hotel Department and a Cruise Department (or Social Department as it may be called). Some of the main types of work available in the Hotel, Catering, Bar and Cruise Departments, and the concessions, are:

Cabin attendants

Cleaners

Restaurant stewards

Bar staff

Galley hands/kitchen porters

Mess stewards (working in the crew dining room)

Hosts/hostesses

Reception desk staff

Chefs (all types)

Retail shop manager

Retail shop assistant

Cashiers.

To get such jobs you usually need to be 20 years old (sometimes minimum 18), of pleasant personality, and have some experience of dealing with the public. (You do not necessarily have to have experience of that particular job).

Finding a job
The best way to finding such work is to make a direct application to the ferry companies and the employment agencies they use. Some of these are listed in Chapter 5. If you fit their basic requirements they will usually interview you and then keep your details on file until a suitable vacancy arises.

Pay and Conditions
The working pattern on board a long haul ferry is typically one week on, one week off, two weeks on, followed by one week off, working 12-hour split shifts. However, it does vary according to the routes the ferry is operating. All accommodation and meals are usually provided

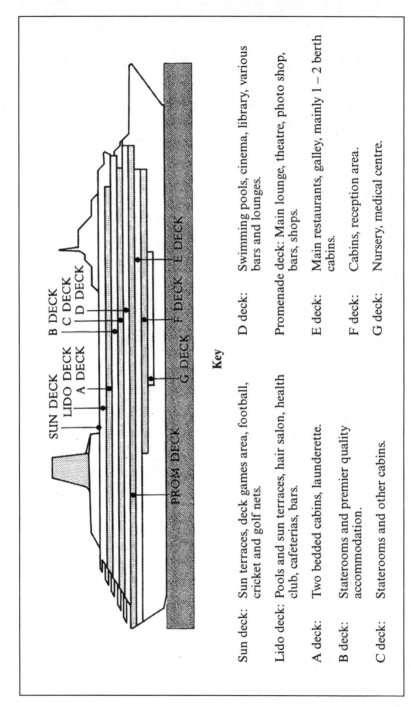

Key

Sun deck: Sun terraces, deck games area, football, cricket and golf nets.

Lido deck: Pools and sun terraces, hair salon, health club, cafeterias, bars.

A deck: Two bedded cabins, launderette.

B deck: Staterooms and premier quality accommodation.

C deck: Staterooms and other cabins.

D deck: Swimming pools, cinema, library, various bars and lounges.

Promenade deck: Main lounge, theatre, photo shop, bars, shops.

E deck: Main restaurants, galley, mainly 1 – 2 berth cabins.

F deck: Cabins, reception area.

G deck: Nursery, medical centre.

Fig. 9. Finding your way round a cruise ship.

whilst you are working. Rates of pay are comparable with similar jobs on dry land.

Contracts for this type of work are usually indefinite rather than being of the fixed-length type as for cruise ships.

If nothing else, working on a ferry will certainly help you decide if this type of work is for you. If you don't like ferry work then you might not be suited to cruise ship work although, of course, with a ferry there are no sun-drenched beaches to enjoy!

4
Jobs You Could Do
on a Cruise Ship

In this chapter we will take a look at some of the main types of work that are available on board cruise ships and also give some advice on how and where to obtain them.

Ship's Officer
What this job involves
The ship's officers are very much the management of the ship and are responsible for its smooth running, especially insofar as navigation, engineering and safety are concerned. The ultimate ship's officer is of course the captain.

The ship's officers are, mainly, either deck officers or engineering officers, although a new designation, the dual certificate officer (which combines both tasks), is becoming more common.

What you need to apply
Applicants must usually have a minimum of three GCSEs or equivalent Scottish qualifications and some companies expect a higher level of qualification (such as five GCSEs plus two A-Levels).

How and where to find vacancies
The most usual method of becoming a ship's officer is to be sponsored on a training scheme by a shipping company or training group. This lasts up to four years and includes periods of college study and sea service. During this time cadets study for a Department of Transport Certificate of Competency at either classes 3, 4 or 5, depending on their qualifications. After further considerable experience those aiming to become a chief officer will require at least a Class 2 Certificate and those aiming to become a ship's master (or captain) a Class 1 Certificate.

Not all shipping companies sponsor trainees. However, as the work is similar no matter what type of ship is involved it is possible to start with any shipping company and later on transfer to the cruise ship business.

Pay and benefits
Pay is in the region of £15,000 for a junior officer, up to £60,000 or more for an experienced captain.   Many officers follow a working pattern of five months' working and two months' leave.

On a cruise ship, unlike other types of vessel, the ship's officers are able, in fact expected, to take an active part in the ship's social scene.

Special tips to help you
Most trainees are in the 16 – 19 age group, up to 25 as a maximum. Training places are highly sought after so early application is advised.

Ship's Rating
What this job involves
Ratings usually undertake skilled and unskilled maintenance, repair and cleaning work both above and below decks.   Traditionally ratings are divided into deck ratings and engine room ratings, although nowadays the distinction is less clear.

What you need to apply
Applicants must usually have at least three GCSEs. The usual route of entry is to be sponsored by a shipping company to take an approved course, such as that run at the National Sea Training College, Gravesend.

How and where to find vacancies
Apply direct to shipping companies, although not all sponsor trainees and competition is fierce for the vacancies that do occur.   Since the work on a cruise ship is almost identical to that on any other large merchant vessel it is possible to first obtain work with any type of shipping company and then later transfer to the cruise ship business.

Pay and benefits
Basic pay plus overtime. Total hours worked may exceed 70 hours per week, depending on what work needs to be done.

Special tips to help you
Most trainees sponsored by shipping companies are in the 16 – 18 age range and early application should be made to stand a chance at securing a place on a course. Sponsors usually look for some evidence of interest in making a career at sea, such as membership of the Sea Cadets.

Carpenter

What this job involves
Providing a maintenance and repair service around the ship.

What you need to apply
Sound experience of all types of joinery, preferably obtained in a busy commercial environment, such as shopfitting. Or to have serviced a full apprenticeship. Minimum age to join a ship is usually 21.

How and where to find vacancies
Apply direct to shipping companies and contractors.

Pay and benefits
Rates of pay are usually in excess of land-based rates but employment may be on a fixed term contract only.

Special tips to help you
Preference is usually given to applicants who have experience of working in a shipyard.

Plumber

What this job involves
Undertaking plumbing maintenance and repairs on the ship's plumbing systems.

What you need to apply
A recognised plumbing qualification, such as NVQs (or SVQs) in Mechanical Engineering Services (Plumbing) at Levels 2 and 3. Or to have served a full apprenticeship. Minimum age usually 21.

How and where to find vacancies
Make enquiries direct with cruise ships and plumbing contractors.

Pay and benefits
Rates of pay are usually in excess of land-based rates but employment may be on a fixed term contract only.

Special tips to help you
It is an advantage to have worked in a shipyard.

Electrician
What this job involves
Providing a maintenance and repair service for domestic and commercial electrical equipment on board the ship. For example, kitchen equipment, cleaning appliances and fruit machines *etc.* This work is distinct from that carried out by the Marine Engineers.

What you need to apply
Applicants should have experience as installation electricians or production electricians plus a recognised qualification such as a relevant NVQ, as a minimum, or even a City & Guilds Joint Certificate of Engineering Craft.

How and where to find vacancies
Make enquiries direct with cruise lines and electrical contractors.

Pay and benefits
Usually in excess of land-based rates but may be on a fixed term contract only.

Special tips to help you
It is an advantage to have worked in a shipyard or dockyard.

Painter
What this job involves
Painting and decorating, paper hanging and French polishing in the public areas and cabins as part of an on-going maintenance process.

What you need to apply
Experience as a painter and decorator with a commercial firm, preferably one involved in high quality decorating.

How and where to find vacancies
Most vacancies of this nature are with either the cruise lines or specialist decorating contractors to whom application should be made.

Pay and benefits
Rates of pay are usually in excess of land-based rates but employment may be on a fixed term contract only.

Special tips to help you
Ship-based experience is not usually necessary but applicants must be experienced in all aspects of the work and be able to work to a very high standard.

Purser
What this job involves
The purser is responsible for the administration on board ship, including finance, payroll, accounting and so on. His staff also provide an information service for passengers and are in overall control of customer care.

What you need to apply
Experience in management or deputy management of a good-quality hotel. Professional qualifications such as a HND or OND in Hotel and Catering Management, or membership of HCIMA (The Hotel, Catering and Institutional Management Association) are usually required but not always essential if you have the correct experience.

How and where to find vacancies
National newspapers, or direct application to cruise lines.

Pay and benefits
Vary according to responsibility involved but are usually comparable with or better than a good-quality hotel.

Special tips to help you
Language skills are a definite advantage.

Purser's Assistant
What this job involves
Assisting the purser in the smooth running of the ship. Main functions include office and administrative work and also manning the purser's office and information desk.

What you need to apply
The minimum requirements are usually five GCSE passes including English and Maths. Professional qualifications such as a HND or OND in Hotel and Catering Management, or membership of HCIMA, are an advantage.

How and where to find vacancies
National press, *Overseas Jobs Express, Caterer and Hotelkeeper*, direct application to cruise lines.

Pay and benefits
Comparable with or better than similar land-based work.

Special tips to help you
Applicants must have a high standard of personal presentation. Language skills (any European language) are helpful. The minimum age required by most cruise lines is 21.

A Day in the Life of ....

Juliet Graham, Assistant Purser

We work an eight hour shift and today I'm working a split shift. This means that I'll be starting at 0800 hours until 12 noon, and then again from 1600 hours to 2000 hours, probably later.

These are the busiest times of day for the job I'm doing at the moment, which is manning the information desk. Our job is generally to help passengers who have queries and see that they are all sorted out satisfactorily. This might include simply giving directions in the lobby, or dealing with a passenger complaint.

My job is especially hectic at the beginning and end of the cruise when all the purser's staff are busy all day either welcoming new passengers or helping to get them all off the ship and on their way home as quickly as possible. It's very satisfying but one drawback is that we don't get to spend much of our free time in the port since they're our busiest days!

Secretary
What this job involves
Typing, wordprocessing and other secretarial work in the ship's office.

What you need to apply
Experience of working in a busy office and a typing/wordprocessing qualification.

How and where to find vacancies
Apply direct to cruise lines and employment agencies.

Pay and benefits
Similar to dry land.

Special tips to help you
The ability to do administrative work and telephone work is useful as this job is often combined with that of office clerk and telephonist. Shorthand and audio typing skills are also an advantage.

Office Clerk
What this job involves
Administrative and secretarial duties for the ship's officers, especially the purser.

What you need to apply
Office staff must be computer literate. Applicants should have experience of working in a busy office. Experience of working as a PA (personal assistant) is useful.

How and where to find vacancies
Vacancies are scarce. Apply direct to cruise lines and employment agencies.

Pay and benefits
Similar to or less than dry land.

Special tips to help you
Language skills are useful although not essential.

Telephone Operator
What this job involves
Operating the ship's switchboard and receiving/placing ship to shore telephone calls.

What you need to apply
Experience as a telephone operator on dry land and a pleasant telephone manner.

How and where to find vacancies
National press, *Overseas Job Express*, direct application to cruise lines and employment agencies.

Pay and benefits
Similar to dry land.

Special tips to help you
Language ability (especially French, German, Spanish, Italian) is an advantage.

Printer
What this job involves
Printing the ship's daily newspaper, bulletins and programmes for passengers, plus commercial stationery for the ship.

What you need to apply
Applicants must be competent in the use of offset litho equipment.

How and where to find vacancies
National press, trade journals, *Overseas Jobs Express*.

Pay and benefits
Similar to dry land.

Special tips to help you
Ideally printers should also know how to carry out minor repairs and overhauls on equipment.

Journalist
What this job involves
Many ships employ a journalist to produce the ship's daily newspaper which gives news about all activities on board that day, plus a digest of world news.

What you need to apply
Applicants should have experience of working on a newspaper or magazine. Minimum age is often 23 or 25.

How and where to find vacancies
Vacancies are quite rare. See the national press or apply direct to cruise lines.

Pay and benefits
Similar to dry land.

Special tips to help you
The ability to use a DTP system is an advantage as journalists often not only write but typeset the ship's newspaper.

Hotel Manager
What this job involves
The hotel manager is responsible for supervising the cabin stewards and ensuring a high standard of service in the passenger accommodation.

What you need to apply
Sound experience of similar work (such as housekeeping) in a good-quality hotel.

How and where to find vacancies
National press, *Overseas Jobs Express*, or approaching the cruise lines and employment agencies direct (see 'Employers' section).

Pay and benefits
Similar to dry land.

Special tips to help you
Vacancies of this type are quite scarce and those interested in applying should have a proven track record in good-quality hotels, preferably well known international establishments.

Cabin Steward
What this job involves
Cabin stewards and stewardesses are responsible for the cleanliness and making up of the passenger cabins and also, in some cases, for providing services such as laundry and room service. They are also expected to help passengers feel at home and help with their queries and problems.

What you need to apply
Experience of similar work (such as a chambermaid or room attendant) in a good-quality hotel. The age range preferred by most cruise lines is 21 – 35 but this is not fixed.

How and where to find vacancies
National press, *Overseas Jobs Express,* or approaching the cruise lines
and employment agencies direct (see 'Employers' section).

Pay and benefits
Basic wage plus tips. Tipping is expected on most cruise lines and
stewards can often double their basic wage this way.

Special tips to help you
A neat appearance and pleasant, helpful personality are essential.
Language skills are useful, but not essential.

A Day in the Life of ....

Sally Ware, Cabin Stewardess

I got this job about three years ago. I'd been working for about six
months as a chambermaid in a four star hotel in Birmingham.
Really the job was going nowhere. I saw an ad for cruise ship jobs
one day and applied. I turned out to have just the sort of experience
they were looking for and this is now the third ship I've worked on!

The backbone of our job is room cleaning and bed-making, but
there's a bit more to it than that. If a passenger needs laundry
service, would like a drink served in their cabin, or has a special
request like fresh flowers for a wedding anniversary then we help
them arrange it. It's worth our while to be as helpful as possible as
we do rely on tips to a certain extent to make up our salary.

My advice to anyone wanting to work on a cruise ship would be –go
on – give it a try. You don't have to take a second contract if you
don't want to. We enjoy ourselves off duty but I would certainly say
that the work I do is harder than in a hotel and we do work longer
hours.

Cleaner
What this job involves
Cleaning the public areas such as the lounges, bars, restaurants, casino,
showroom and deck areas.

What you need to apply
Applicants should be able to use commercial cleaning equipment and have carried out this work in a commercial environment which demands a high quality of work.

How and where to find vacancies
Apply direct to cruise lines.

Pay and benefits
Similar to/less than on dry land but with all food and accommodation provided.

Special tips to help you
Cleaners should be of neat appearance and pleasant personality. Similar work is also carried out by utility stewards.

Chef
What this job involves
Most cruise ships employ an army of chefs, from the head chef who plans the menus and ensures the food is always of an excellent standard to the sous chefs, chefs de partie and commis chefs who do the actual food preparation. The work is identical to that in a hotel or restaurant.

What you need to apply
Applicants must have undertaken a similar position in a good-quality hotel or restaurant on dry land. Professional qualifications (such as City & Guilds 706 or NVQ in Food Preparation and Cooking) are usually required.

How and where to find vacancies
National newspapers, *Caterer & Hotelkeeper*, direct application to cruise lines and employment agencies (see Chapter 5).

Pay and benefits
Vary according to skills, qualifications and experience.

Special tips to help you
The minimum age to become a chef on a cruise ship is typically 23, but do check with individual employers as this varies.

Kitchen Porter
What this job involves
Kitchen porters do unskilled and semi-skilled work in the galley such as handling the stores, vegetable preparation, dishwashing and cleaning.

What you need to apply
Experience of doing the job in a hotel, restaurant or institutional kitchen.

How and where to find vacancies
National newspapers, *Caterer & Hotelkeeper*, direct application to cruise lines and employment agencies (see 'Employers' section).

Pay and benefits
Similar to/less than land-based work with all food and accommodation provided.

Special tips to help you
Note that many cruise lines mainly employ unskilled labour from low wage countries (such as those in the Far East) for this and other types of unskilled work.

Restaurant Manager
What this job involves
Several restaurant managers (and assistant managers) are employed on most ships to ensure the smooth running of the restaurant including organising seating plans, seating passengers and dealing with enquiries and complaints.

What you need to apply
Experience of working in a good-quality restaurant is essential.

How and where to find vacancies
National newspapers, *Caterer & Hotelkeeper*, direct application to cruise lines and employment agencies (see 'Employers' section).

Pay and benefits
Negotiable, depending on skills and experience.

Special tips to help you
Most cruise ships also employ people from a similar background to work as *maitre d'hôtel*, which mainly involves greeting-and-seating in the restaurant.

Restaurant Waiter/Steward
What this job involves
Also known as stewards, waiters serve the meals in the ship's restaurants (there can be several on a large ship). Waiters often working in two-man teams consisting of a waiter and a commis waiter.

What you need to apply
Sound experience in a good-quality hotel or restaurant. Waiters must usually have silver service experience and be able to work to the highest standards of presentation.

How and where to find vacancies
National newspapers, *Caterer & Hotelkeeper*, direct application to cruise lines and employment agencies (see 'Employers' section).

Pay and benefits
Pay is usually less than in land-based work but many waiters double their salary with tips.

Special tips to help you
Language knowledge (especially French or Italian) would be an advantage. The age range preferred by many cruise lines is 21 – 35. Although men are traditionally recruited for this work many cruise lines now also engage women too.

A Day in the Life of ....

Andrew Mates, Restaurant Steward

I started this job last year. I got it by writing a letter, and sending my CV, to every cruise line I could think of. I didn't hear anything from most of them but three gave me an interview and I had two job offers which I was quite pleased about.

The work here is very much like working in a restaurant in a good quality hotel. In fact, that's where most of use restaurant stewards used to work before. Because, on a ship, the restaurant must open every day we have to work almost every lunchtime and evening. The good thing though is that once lunch is finished we have most afternoons off. This is great for us since this ship visits a new port almost every day.

The things I like about my job are the good team spirit and the fact that, since food and accommodation is free, we can save most of our wages and tips. One the minus side, our crew cabins are a bit small and you don't really get much time for yourself. It's great for single people but some of the married crew find it a bit of a strain.

Wine Waiter
What this job involves
The wine waiters advise passengers on their wine selection and also ensure their order is properly served.

What you need to apply
Experience as a wine waiter in a good-quality hotel or restaurant. A professional qualification, such as those offered by the Academy of Wine Service, Court of Master Sommeliers or Wine and Spirit Education Trust, would be an advantage but is not essential.

How and where to find vacancies
National newspapers, *Caterer & Hotelkeeper*, direct application to cruise lines and employment agencies (see 'Employers' section).

Pay and benefits
Similar to comparable land-based work.

Special tips to help you
Wine waiters must have an extensive and professional knowledge of the world's wines.

Barman/woman
What this job involves
Most cruise ships have a large number of bars in the many lounges, showrooms and casinos. The barmen and women serve the public directly and also make up orders for the cocktail waiters.

What you need to apply
Experience of bar work in a good-quality hotel or restaurant and a knowledge of all kinds of drinks including cocktails. A qualification such as City & Guilds 707 (Parts I & II) or NVQs (National Vocational Qualifications) in Catering & Hospitality (Serving Food & Drink – Bar) at Levels 1 and 2 is an advantage.

How and where to find vacancies
National newspapers, *Overseas Jobs Express, Caterer & Hotelkeeper*, direct application to cruise lines and employment agencies (see 'Employers' section).

Pay and benefits
Similar to/slightly less than on dry land. May also receive tips.

Special tips to help you
A pleasant personality and high standard of appearance are an advantage.

Cocktail Waiter
What this job involves
Cocktail waiters wait on passengers in the lounges, showrooms and casinos.

What you need to apply
Experience of this kind of work in a good-quality hotel or similar.

How and where to find vacancies
National newspapers, *Overseas Jobs Express, Caterer & Hotelkeeper*, direct application to cruise lines and employment agencies (see 'Employers' section).

Pay and benefits
Similar to/slightly less than comparable land-based work.

Special tips to help you
A pleasant personality and smart appearance are essential.

Cruise Director
What this job involves
The cruise director is responsible for organising and supervising all the

onboard entertainment activities from daytime sporting activities to the very extensive programme of evening entertainment that most ships feature.

What you need to apply
Extensive experience in the leisure and entertainment industry.

How and where to find vacancies
As vacancies are few interested parties should make an approach direct to the cruise lines.

Pay and benefits
Negotiable.

Special tips to help you
Would-be cruise directors must have real enthusiasm for the position and be able to show a sound track record in successfully organising programmes of entertainment.

Cruise Department Staff
What this job involves
The cruise department staff (or cruise assistants) organise – and take part in – a full programme of day and evening activities, such as sporting events, competitions, parties, dances and floorshows *etc*. They also generally act as hosts/hostesses to ensure that the passengers enjoy their cruise.

What you need to apply
Experience in a related field, such as the leisure industry, hotel industry, entertainment industry or as a holiday courier.

How and where to find vacancies
Apply direct to the cruise lines and employment agencies. Also see the national press, and *The Stage and Television Today* newspaper.

Pay and benefits
Vary according to experience.

Special tips to help you
Language skills are an advantage but not essential. A high standard of appearance and pleasant personality is a must.

A Day in the Life of....

Nina Sharpe, Cruise Assistant

My day starts in the afternoon when I'll be running a bingo session in the lounge. As soon as it's finished I'll have to nip down to the ballroom to get the afternoon tea dance underway. This is very popular and it's my job to co-ordinate both the band and the catering so that everything runs smoothly and also generally act as a hostess.

After a quick bite to eat I'll be hosting our singles party, which we hold at the beginning of the cruise for people who are travelling alone. Then, I'll be mingling at the Captain's cocktail party.

Socialising sounds like fun but actually it's very hard work, especially when you have to make sure you keep a smile on your face all the time, even when you don't feel like it.

Prior to applying for this job I was a package holiday courier and think that the experience of meeting, greeting and helping people is one of the best qualifications you can have for this type of job.

Entertainer (Singer/Dancer/Musician *etc*)
What this job involves
Most cruise ships offer a full programme of entertainment every night and all types of entertainers are required. Many ships have a full-sized showroom offering Las Vegas style productions and some also have a theatre.

What you need to apply
You must be able to sing, dance or play an instrument to a good professional standard. Groups and duos are also employed.

How and where to find vacancies
Make direct approaches to the cruise lines and theatrical employment agencies (see Chapter 5). *The Stage and Television Today* newspaper is also a very good source of vacancies.

Pay and benefits
Varies according to skills/experience. Entertainers may be hired for a season, a single cruise, or just for a single performance.

Special tips to help you
Would-be entertainers must have a polished, professional act and be able to pass a very demanding audition.

Children's Host/ess

What this job involves
The children's hosts and hostesses look after children aged up to 16 and ensure they have an enjoyable time by organising events such as sporting activities, parties, discos, quizzes and competitions.

What you need to apply
Experience of working with and/or teaching young children is needed. A professional qualification (such as the NNEB Diploma) is an advantage.

How and where to find vacancies
Apply direct to cruise lines. Also see national press and *Overseas Jobs Express*.

Pay and benefits
Vary according to responsibilities involved.

Special tips to help you
You must genuinely like children to succeed in this job.

Children's Entertainer

What this job involves
Entertaining children, usually of an age range between 5 and 16.

What you need to apply
Applicants should have experience of entertaining children and have a repertoire of acts they can perform (for example, magic tricks, singing or whatever).

How and where to find vacancies
Direct application to employers.

Pay and benefits
Vary, depending on skills and qualifications.

Special tips to help you

Children's hosts and entertainers are usually only employed by those cruise lines which attract families. Lines which attract upmarket or older passengers do not have a requirement for crew of this type.

Children's Nanny

What this job involves

The children's nannies look after children in the daytime creche and also organise babysitting at night.

What you need to apply

Experience of working with babies and children is a must. An NNEB Diploma or other childcare qualification is an advantage.

How and where to find vacancies

National newspapers, *The Lady* magazine.

Pay and benefits

Similar to or less than comparable work on dry land.

Special tips to help you

Children's nannies must genuinely enjoy this type of work. The minimum age is normally 23.

Disc Jockey (DJ)

What this job involves

Most ships have a disco and many also a nightclub offering an atmosphere and standard of music comparable with a top land-based club.

What you need to apply

Experience of DJ work in a good-quality establishment, extensive knowledge of all types of music and a pleasant personality.

How and where to find vacancies

National newspapers and direct application to employers.

Pay and benefits

Depend on skill and experience. The best DJs earn excellent wages. DJs are allowed to use all the ship's facilities and mix with the passengers.

Special tips to help you
DJs must have a very high standard of professionalism.

Doctor
What this job involves
Every ship has a well-equipped medical centre which can deal with both minor ailments and emergencies.

What you need to apply
At least three years' post qualification experience particularly in A&E, ICU and CCU.

How and where to find vacancies
Vacancies are scarce as most ships have only one or two doctors. Interested parties should contact cruise ships direct.

Pay and benefits
Negotiable. The positioning of ship's doctor always carries a great deal of prestige.

Special tips to help you
Applicants should usually be ALC certified.

Nurse
What this job involves
Every ship has a well-equipped medical centre which can deal with both minor ailments and emergencies. The ship's nurses are required to assist the doctor, carry out routine procedures such as immunisations, and also administer first aid when required.

What you need to apply
Applicants must be Registered General Nurses and preferably hold an ALS certificate. Experience in A&E, ICU, theatre duties and private medicine is an advantage.

How and where to find vacancies
Make direct approaches to the cruise lines.

Pay and benefits
Rates of pay normally exceed rates on dry land.

Special tips to help you
Ship's nurses are usually in the 25 – 40 age group but there is no fixed limit.

Shop Manager
What this job involves
Most ships have a range of shops such as a general store, pharmacy, fashion boutique, gift shop and duty free boutique. The QE2 has a branch of the famous London store Harrods!

What you need to apply
Applicants must have sound retail management knowledge preferably obtained in a good-quality retail outlet.

How and where to find vacancies
National newspapers, direct application to cruise lines and concessionaires.

Pay and benefits
Basic pay plus commission.

Special tips to help you
Shop managers must have a strong commercial awareness and be able to contribute to the profitability of their outlets.

Shop Assistant
What this job involves
Most ships have a range of shops such as a general store, pharmacy, fashion boutique, gift shop and duty free boutique. These are often run by concessionaires rather than the cruise line itself.

What you need to apply
Experience of working in a good-quality retail outlet such as a jewellers, fashion boutique, department store or perfumer.

How and where to find vacancies
Direct application to the concessionaires and/or cruise lines.

Pay and benefits
Shop assistants receive a small basic wage and bonus/commission for meeting specified sales targets.

Special tips to help you
Language skills (French, German, Italian) are an advantage for this type of work, although not essential.

Photographer
What this job involves
Every ship has a number of resident photographers who take photographs of passengers during the cruise and then offer them for sale in the photo shop.

What you need to apply
Applicants must be experienced professional photographers. The ability to develop and print photographs is also sometimes required.

How and where to find vacancies
Most photographers are employed by concessionaires and direct application should be made to them (see Chapter 5).

Pay and benefits
Pay is either basic wage plus commission or commission-only in some cases.

Photographers are able to use all the ship's facilities and mix with the passengers.

Special tips to help you
Photographers should actually enjoy their work and have good selling skills.

A Day in the Life of ....

Duncan Wright, Ship's Photographer

I came to this job with no experience of professional photography. I'd always been what I considered a 'good amateur' and had a very extensive portfolio of work, including weddings which are excellent training for this job. When I saw jobs for photographers advertised I just applied and was lucky enough to be successful.

Most days I work a few hours in the afternoon and a few hours in the evening. Most of my time is spent snapping the passengers around the ship. Then I develop the photos (the ship has its own automatic processing equipment) and sell them in the photo shop. Everybody wants a photo with the captain at the Captain's Reception!

My job is probably one of the easiest on board. I work fairly short hours — actually I can set my own hours and, when I'm not working, I live very much like the passengers on the ship do, which is great. I don't work for the cruise line but for a concessionaire. They pay the cruise line for the right to operate the photo shop.

My advice to anyone wanting to work on a ship? Try, try and keep trying. And don't wait for a job to be advertised — send out your CV to as many employers as you can find.

Casino Croupier
What this job involves
Most ships have a very large casino and a large number of croupiers is required to conduct games such as roulette.

What you need to apply
Croupiers must have at least one year's experience of working in a land -based casino. This can be obtained by applying for a trainee's position with a city-centre casino.

How and where to find vacancies
Many casinos are run by concessionaires and croupiers should apply to these concessionaires or to shipboard employment agencies (see 'Employers' section).

Pay and benefits
Pay is similar to land-based work and croupiers are also often paid bonuses, as well as receiving tips.

Special tips to help you
Croupiers must be of smart appearance and pleasant personality. Minimum age is usually 21 but this does vary.

Cashier
What this job involves
Providing a *bureau de change* service exchanging foreign currency for passengers and administering the passenger accounts.

What you need to apply
Experience of working in a bank or *bureau de change* or similar.

How and where to find vacancies
Apply direct to cruise lines (see 'Employers' section later in this book.)

Pay and benefits
Comparable with dry land.

Special tips to help you
Language skills are useful but not essential.

Tour Guide

What this job involves
Tour guides organise, sell and conduct the excursions which cruise ships operate in almost every port of call.

What you need to apply
A professional tour guiding qualification would be an advantage, as would experience of working as a tour guide or holiday courier.

How and where to find vacancies
National newspapers, direct application to cruise lines.

Pay and benefits
Tour guides are usually paid a commission on excursions sold.

Special tips to help you
Good marketing skills (*ie* the ability to sell excursions) and language skills (French, German, Spanish) would be an advantage for this type of work.

Sports Instructor

What this job involves
Conducting sports lessons and supervising sporting activities. Most ships offer a very wide range of sporting activities such as waterskiing, scuba diving, windsurfing, swimming, shooting, tennis, football *etc*.

What you need to apply
Applicants should have a coaching qualification (any type) in several different sports.

How and where to find vacancies
National newspapers, direct applications to cruise lines.

Pay and benefits
Similar to dry land. Sports instructors are usually able to use all the ship's facilities and mix with the passengers.

Special tips to help you
Applicants should be experienced in as many different sports as possible.

Beauty Therapist
What this job involves
Most ships have a beauty salon (sometimes connected with the hair salon) and offer a very extensive range of facials, make-up service, manicures and pedicures.

What you need to apply
Therapists must have a professional qualification (any kind) and at least one to two years' experience in a land-based beauty salon.

How and where to find vacancies
National newspapers and by applying direct to concessionaires such as Steiner (see Chapter 5).

Pay and benefits
Small basic wage plus tips and commission on beauty products sold in the salon.

Special tips to help you
Therapists must have a high standard of presentation and customer care. Selling skills are also desirable.

Gym Instructor
What this job involves
Gym instructors are employed to run the gym and also to conduct lessons in keep fit, aerobics and similar leisure activities.

What you need to apply
Experience of working in a land-based gym, leisure or sports centre. A qualification such as RSA Exercise to Music would be an advantage.

How and where to find vacancies
National newspapers, employment agencies.

Pay and benefits
Similar to land-based jobs.

Special tips to help you
Gym instructors should be experienced in as wide a range of exercises and sports as possible.

Masseur/se
What this job involves
Massage staff provide a professional massage service on board and also run the sauna, steam room and health spa facilities that are found on board ship.

What you need to apply
A professional massage qualification (any) is desirable, either in therapeutic or sports massage.

How and where to find vacancies
National newspapers, employment agencies, concessionaires.

Pay and benefits
Comparable to land-based jobs. Masseur/ses depend to some extent on tips.

Special tips to help you
Shipboard massage staff must practise the highest standard of professionalism and have excellent customer care skills.

Hairdresser
What this job involves
The hair salon is a very important service on any cruise ship and usually busy all day, every day.

What you need to apply
Those wishing to work on a shipboard salon should be competent stylists with at least one to two years' experience in a good-quality city-centre hair salon.

How and where to find vacancies
National newspapers, *Overseas Jobs Express, Hairdresser's Journal International.* Also apply to concessionaires such as Steiner (see Chapter 5).

Pay and benefits
Small basic salary plus tips/commission.

Special tips to help you
Shipboard stylists must have very high standards of presentation and customer care skills.

A Day in the Life of ....

Mary Ann Martin, Hair Stylist

I got my job by replying to an ad in the *Overseas Jobs Express.* Actually, most of the concessionaires operating hair salons have vacancies nearly all the time, so if anyone is interested in this type of work I suggest they send them their CV.

The work here is not too demanding in that ladies come into the salon just to keep their hair looking perfect for the following evening, rather than for a complete restyle. Our salon is really posh though and everything has to be done by the book.

There's a great team spirit on board and work is only minutes from 'home', so it's much nicer than working in a city-centre salon. The salon closes in the early evening so we have every night off. Because we're open every day we don't get many full days off but I've managed to spend some time in every port we've visited on this route.

5
Employers You Can Apply To

The companies listed in this chapter include cruise and ferry lines, concessionaires and employment agencies. Please refer to the individual entry to see what type of jobs are available and on what basis they are likely to be offered.

CRUISE LINES, CONCESSIONAIRES AND AGENCIES

Abercrombie & Kent
1520 Kensington Road, Oak Brook, IL60521, USA.

A small cruise line which specialises in adventure cruising, mainly to areas with rare and unusual wildlife.

ACCL (American Canadian Caribbean Line)
461 Water Street, PO Box 368, Warren, RI02885, USA.
Tel: 401 247 0955.

This cruise line cruises in the Caribbean in the winter and the waters around Canada in the summer. It operates two 'mini cruise ships' which are designed so as to be able to dock on beaches.

Airtours
Wavell House, Holcombe Road, Helmshore, Rosendale, Lancs BB4 4NB. Tel: (01706) 240033.

Having first operated in 1995 this cruise line is owned by the Airtours holiday company and specialises in offering fly-cruise holidays mainly in the Mediterranean.

All jobs other than entertainers should apply to their employment agency: V Ships, Aigue Marine, 24 avenue de Fontvieille, PO Box 639, MC98013, Monaco.

Allders International (Ships) Limited
84 – 98 Southampton Road, Eastleigh, Hants SO5 5ZF.
   In USA: 1510 SE 17th Street, Fort Lauderdale, FL33316, USA.

   Allders operates duty free and gift shops on board numerous ships
   on a concessionary basis. They employ experienced retail staff.

Ambassador Cruises
Box 157, Limassol, Cyprus.

   A small cruise line which is based in Cyprus. Mostly Cypriot/Greek
   crew.

American Hawaii Cruises
550 Kearney Street, San Francisco, CA94108, USA. Tel: 415 392
   9400.

   American Hawaii Cruises operates cruises around the Hawaiian
   Islands.   Note: for operational reasons employment is mainly
   restricted to US nationals only.

Apollo Ship Chandlers
900 NW 43rd Street, Miami, FL33166, USA.

   Apollo operates shops and concessionary bar/café facilities on
   Florida-based ships. They employ shop assistants, bar and catering
   staff.

Atlantic Associates
990 NW 166th Street, Miami, FL33126, USA.

   Agency providing casino staff for Miami-based cruises. Employs
   experienced croupiers and other casino staff.

Ausonia Cruises
Via C D'Andrea, 80133 Naples, Italy. Tel: 115 0673.

   Ausonia is a one-ship Italian cruise line offering short cruises in the
   Mediterranean.

Berkeley Bureau
11 Cranmer Road, Hampton Hill, Middlesex TW12 1DW.

An employment agency which hires croupiers for the casinos on board cruise ships.

Berkeley Scott Selection
11 – 13 Ockford Road, Godalming, Surrey GU7 1QU. Tel: (01483) 414141.

An employment agency which recruits for the hotel and catering industry and has a small number of opportunities, mainly for chefs on board ships.

BLASCO: Black Sea Shipping Company Limited
1 Ulitsa Lastochkina, Odessa, Ukraine. Tel: 0482 252160.

BLASCO operates 14 cruise ships and cruises all around the world. Although most of the crew are Ukrainian they charter their ships to western operators and so employ some western cruise department staff, especially German speaking.

Carnival Cruise Lines
Alton House, 177 High Holborn, London WC2R 0PT. Tel: (0171) 240 3336.
USA: 3665 NW 87th Avenue, Miami, FL33178, USA. Tel: 305 599 2600.

Carnival is a US cruise line but employs crew from many nationalities. It has expanded rapidly since it began operations in 1972 and now operates 14 ships. UK-based applicants should apply to the London office.

Casinos Austria International
35 Dover Street, London W1X 3RA.
USA: 555 NE 15th Street, Plaza Venetia, Miami, FL33132, USA.
Casinos Austria International runs casinos on a concessionary basis, although not all of their vacancies are on board ships.

Celebrity Cruises
95 Akti Miaouli, 18538 Piraeus, Athens, Greece.
  USA: 5200 Blue Lagoon Drive, Miami, FL33126, USA. Tel: 314
  727 2929.

Although Celebrity is a Greek company its ships are mostly based
in the Caribbean for US passengers and so many English-speaking
crew members are recruited.

Classical Cruise Line
132 E 70th Street, New York, NY10021, USA.

A small cruise line which operates speciality cruises to historic
locations.

Clipper Cruise Line
7710 Bonhomme Avenue, St Louis, MO63105, USA.

Clipper operates cruises along the coast of the USA and in the
Caribbean with three small ships.

Club Mediterranee
Service Recrutement, Frankrijklei 49, B2000 Antwerp, Belgium.

The Club Med cruise line is owned by the same company which
operates Club Med holiday villages. It operates two small-scale sail
cruise ships.

Commodore Cruise Line
800 Douglas Road, Suite 700, Coral Gables, FL33114, USA. Tel: 800
237 5361.

This US cruise line operates in the Caribbean in the winter and the
waters around Canada in the summer.

Costa Cruises
Via G d'Annunzio, PO Box 389, Genoa, Italy.

Costa is a long established Italian line (employing a multinational
crew) operating seven ships.

Crews International
Dormer House, Berrynarbor, Devon EX34 9SE. Tel: (01271) 883209.

An employment agency, mainly employing waiters.

Cruise Line Appointments
142 Parkwood Road, Bournemouth BH5 2BW. Tel: (01202) 433464.
Also at Park North Suite 1, 5117 Castello Drive, Naples, Florida
34703 USA.

An employment agency which deals in a variety of positions.

Cruise Picture Co
Suite 817, 330 Biscayne Boulevard, Miami, F133132, USA.

Operates photo-shop concessions on board ships and hires
experienced photographers.

Crystal Cruises
2121 Avenue of the Stars, Los Angeles, CA90067, USA. Tel: 310 785 9300.

Crystal specialises in up-market, luxury cruising using two ships.

CTC Cruise Lines
1 Regent Street, London SW1Y 4NN. Tel: (0171) 930 9963.

CTC is a Ukrainian cruise line but it offers a wide range of cruises
from the UK. As a result it recruits a small number of staff, mainly
for the Cruise Department, in the UK.

CTI Group
1535 SE 17th Street, Fort Lauderdale, FL33316, USA.
Tel: 954 728 9975. Fax: 954 728 9697.

Employs a variety of staff for cruise lines

Cunard Line Limited
South Western House, Canute Road, Southampton SO14 3NR.
Tel: (01703) 716500.
USA: Cunard Line, Entertainment Dept, 555 5th Avenue, New
York, NY10017.

Cunard is the largest British cruise line and is famous worldwide for its flagship, QE2.   Applications for Hotel, Catering and Bar Department ratings should be sent to their employment agency, Logbridge Ltd (see under 'Logbridge').

Delta Marine Personnel Services
36 Spital Square, London E1 6DY. Tel: (0171) 377 0349.

Employment agency for deck and engineering crew only on all types of merchant ships.

Discovery Cruises
1850 Eller Drive, Suite 402, Fort Lauderdale, FL33316, USA. Tel: 305 525 7800.

Discovery operates one ship and runs day-long pleasure cruises from Port Everglades in Florida to the Bahamas and back.

Disney Cruise Line
210 Celebration Place, Celebration, FL34747, USA.

Owned by the Disney Corporation and offers cruises in conjunction with holidays at Walt Disney resorts. Operates two ships.

Dolphin Cruise Line
901 South America Way, Miami, FL33132, USA. Tel: 305 358 5122.

Offers cruises around the Caribbean from Florida with its three ships.

Fantasy Cruises
95 Akti Miaouli, 18538 Piraeus, Athens, Greece.

Recruits internationally, although most senior crew members are Greek.

Fred Olsen Lines
Fred Olsen House, White House Road, Ipswich, Suffolk IP1 5LL.

Fred Olsen cruises in the Mediterranean and Baltic and attracts a large number of British passengers to its two-ship fleet.

G L Productions
1922 NE 149th Street, New York, NY33181, USA.

Provides entertainers for cruise ships.

Greyhound Leisure Services
8052 NW 14th Street, Miami, FL33126–2355, USA. Tel: 305 592 6460.

Operates ship's shops on a concessionary basis. Employs shop assistants and shop management.

Hapag Lloyd
Ballindamm, PO Box 102626, 2000 Hamburg 1, Germany.

A German cruise line. Applicants must speak good German.

Hebridean Island Cruises
Acorn Park, Skipton, North Yorkshire BD23 2UE.

A small UK line which offers tours around the Scottish islands using a small cruiser.

Holland America Line
300 Elliott Avenue West, Seattle, WA98119, USA. Tel: 206 281 3535.

One of the world's largest cruise lines, with seven large ships. Recruits a multinational crew although many crew members are either Dutch or Indonesian.

Info Cruise
PO Box 23195, 1100DR Amsterdam, Netherlands

Employment agency.

Intercruise
126 Kolokotroni Street, 18535 Piraeus, Greece.

A small Greek cruise line operating just one ship.

International Cruise Shops
PO Box 592355, Miami, FL33159, USA.

Operates shop concessions on cruise ships.   Employs retail associates (managers and assistants).

John Leith Oceanic Associates
77 Montem Road, Forest Hill, London SE23 1SH.

An employment agency hiring Cruise Department staff, entertainers, casino staff, pursers, children's hosts/hostesses.

Kristina Cruises
Korkeavuorenkatu 2, 48100 Kotka, Finland.

Finland's main cruise line. Applicants should normally speak a Scandinavian language.

Link Shipping Staff Consultants
10 Minories, London EC3N 1BJ. Tel: (0171) 481 8666.

Employment agency recruiting deck and engineering crew only for all types of merchant ships.

Logbridge Limited
Saxon Gate, Back of the Walls, Southampton, Hants SO14 3NR.
 Tel: (01703) 631331.

Logbridge is an employment agency mainly recruiting Catering, Bar and Hotel Department ratings for Cunard and Seabourn cruise lines.

Louis Cruise Lines
PO Box 5612, Limassol, Cyprus.

This cruise line operates four ferries/cruise ships in the eastern Mediterranean. Crew are multinational.

Majesty Cruise Line
901 South America Way, Miami, FL33132, USA. Tel: 305 532 7788.

Operates one ship, running upmarket cruises.

Marcello Productions
230 SW 8th Street, Miami, FL32130, USA.

An employment agency for entertainers.

Marquest
101 Columbia Street, Suite 150, Laguna Beach, CA92656, USA.

Marquest is a small cruise line which runs adventure and 'nature exploration' cruises.

Meyer Davis Agency
West 57th Street, New York, NY10019, USA.

An employment agency for musicians.

MMSL
Kristen 20, A-6094 Axams, Austria.

An employment agency recruiting crew worldwide.

MSC (Mediterranean Shipping Cruises)
Piazza del Martiri, 80121 Naples, Italy.

Operates three ships cruising in the Mediterranean.

Navigestion
Le Schuylkil, 19 Boulevard de Suisse, Monte Carlo 9800, Monaco.
Tel: 92 16 07 87.

An employment agency. Applicants should be French-speakers.

Norwegian Cruise Line
7665 Corporate Centre Drive, Miami FL33126, USA.

One of the largest cruise lines. NCL is Norwegian owned but operates extensively in the USA.

NYK Cruises
Yusen Building, 3-2 Marunouchi 2-chome, Chiyoda-ku, Tokyo, Japan.

NYK is a Japanese cruise line with a single-ship fleet. Many ratings in the Hotel, Catering and Bar Department are European and the ship does carry English-speaking passengers. However, applicants should speak Japanese.

Ocean Cruise Lines
5 Boulevard Malesherbes, 75008 Paris, France. Tel: 1 49 24 42 00.

Ocean Cruise Lines is a French cruise line operating a single ship in the Caribbean.

Ocean Images
7 Home Farm, Lockerley Hall, Romsey, Hants SO51 0JT.

Ocean employs on-board photographers.

Orient Lines
1510 SE 17th St, Fort Lauderdale, FL33316, USA. Tel: 305 527 6660.

Orient operates a single-ship cruising worldwide but frequently in the Far East.

P&O Cruises Limited
Richmond House, Terminus Terrace, Southampton, Hants SO14 3PN. Tel: (01703) 534200.
USA: 10100 Santa Monica Boulevard, Los Angeles, CA90067-4189, USA.

P&O is one of Britain's most well known shipping companies which now operates three cruise ships.

Pacquet French Cruises
5 Boulevard Malesherbes, 75008 Paris, France. Tel: 1 49 24 42 00.

Pacquet is a French cruise line. Non-French applicants may apply but they must speak excellent French.

Paradise Cruises
PO Box 157, Limassol, Cyprus.

A small single-ship Cypriot cruise line.

Premier Cruises
400 Challenger Road, Cape Canaveral, FL32920, USA. Tel: 407 783 5061.

Premier offers three and four day cruises from Florida ports.

Princess Boutiques
10100 Santa Monica Boulevard, Los Angeles, CA90067-4189, USA.
Operates shops on board Princess Cruises ships. Hires shop
assistants and managers.

Princess Casinos
10100 Santa Monica Boulevard, Los Angeles, CA90067-4189, USA.

Operates casinos on board Princess Cruises ships. Hires croupiers.

Princess Cruises
10100 Santa Monica Boulevard, Los Angeles, CA90067-4189, USA.
UK: Richmond House, Terminus Terrace, Southampton, Hants
SO14 3PN. Tel: (01703) 534200.

Princess Cruises is owned by the British shipping company P&O but
it operates its ships mainly in and around the US, catering for
American passengers.   Applications for Hotel Department
vacancies can be made to P&O in the UK (see 'P&O').

Quest SHR
4 – 6 High Street, Eastleigh, Hants SO50 5LA. Tel: (01703) 644933.

Quest SHR is an employment agency which recruits crew members
for ferries rather than cruise ships.

Radisson Seven Seas
600 Corporate Drive, Suite 410, Fort Lauderdale, FL33334, USA. Tel:
305 776 6123.

A two-ship fleet (one of which is a twin-hulled vessel or catamaran)
which specialises in upmarket cruising.   Recruits crew
internationally.

Regal Cruises
4199 34th St South, Suite B-103, St Petersburg, FL33711, USA.

A single-ship cruise line cruising in the Caribbean and east coast
USA.

Renaissance Cruises
Suite 300, 1800 Eller Drive, PO Box 350307, Fort Lauderdale, FL33335-0307, USA. Tel: 303 463 0982.
This line has eight small cruise ships and is Italian owned. However, it operates extensively in the USA and has multinational crews.

RG International
7 Buckland Road, Maidstone, Kent ME16 0SJ.

An employment agency providing Hotel Department staff to cruise lines as well as hotel industry on dry land.

Roger James Music
45 West Street, Los Angeles, CA90039, USA.

This agency provides musicians (all types) for cruise ships.

Royal Caribbean Cruise Line
1050 Caribbean Way, Miami, FL33132, USA. Tel: 305 539 6000.

Royal Caribbean is a very large Norwegian cruise line. However, its main cruising arenas are the Caribbean and most of its passengers are English-speaking and its crew are recruited internationally.

Royal Olympic Cruises
87 Akti Miaouli, 18538 Piraeus, Athens, Greece.

Royal Olympic is a newly formed cruise line which operates six ships mainly on Mediterranean cruises. Although a Greek company its ships have a multinational crew.

Royal Viking Line
95 Merrick Way, Coral Gables, FL33134, USA. Tel: 305 447 9660.

This line operates two luxury cruise ships. The ships are usually based in Europe in the summer and the Caribbean during the winter. RVL is a Norwegian company but hires a multinational crew.

Sea Chest Associates
7385 West Roadway, New Orleans, USA.

Sea Chest runs shops on board ships and recruits retail sales assistants and managers.

Sea Escape Cruises
8751 W Broward Boulevard, Plantation, FL33324, USA. Tel: 305 476 999.

Sea Escape operates one-day 'cruises to nowhere' from Florida ports.

Seabourn Cruise Line
55 Francisco Street, San Francisco, CA94133, USA. Tel: 415 391 7444.

Seabourn operates two small, super-luxury cruise ships which sail in various parts of the world. See also 'Logbridge'.

Seawind Cruise Line
1750 Coral Way, Miami, FL33145, USA.

Seawind cruises the Caribbean all year.

Seven Seas Cruise Line
2-9-1 Nishi-Shinbashi, Minato-Ku, Tokyo, Japan.
    USA: 333 Market Street, Suite 2600, San Francisco, CA94105, USA. Tel: 415 905 6000.

Seven Seas is a Japanese cruise line operating one ship. However, passengers are drawn from all nations and so the crew is multinational.

Silversea Cruises
110 E Broward Boulevard, Fort Lauderdale, FL33301, USA. Tel: 305 522 4477.

Silversea operates two luxury cruise ships cruising in the Baltic, Caribbean and South America.

Southern Games
202 Fulham Road, London SW10 9NB.

Hires casino staff for shipboard casinos.

Special Expeditions
720 5th Avenue, New York, NY10019, USA.

Special Expeditions operates adventure cruises. Their ships are small, so as to be able to visit the smallest ports.

Star Clippers
4010 Salzedo Avenue, Coral Gables, FL33146, USA. Tel: 305 442 0550.

Operates two sail cruise ships.

Steiner Training Limited
57/65 The Broadway, Stanmore, Middlesex HA7 4DU. Tel: (0181) 954 6121.
USA: Steiner Transocean, 1007 N America Way, 4th Floor, Miami, FL33132, USA.

Steiner operates hair and beauty salons and gyms on board ship. They employ hairdressers, beauty therapists, massage staff and gym instructors.

Suncoast Cruise Services
2335 NW 107th Avenue, Miami, FL33172, USA.

Suncoast operates shop concessions on board ship and employs shop assistants and managers.

Swan Hellenic Limited
77 New Oxford Street, London WC1A 1PP. Tel: (0171) 800 2345.

Swan Hellenic is a specialist cruise line which does not operate its own ships but charters them from other companies as needed. Some of their staff work both in the office and on cruise ships during the season.

Thomson
Greater London House, Hampstead Road, London NW1 7SD. Tel: (0171) 383 1080.

The Thomson cruise line started operations in 1996 and runs three ships.

Trans Ocean Photo
711 12th Avenue, New York, NY10019, USA.

Trans Ocean operates photo-shop concessions on board cruise ships.

V Ships
Aigue Marine, 24 avenue de Fontvieille, PO Box 639, MC98013, Monaco.

Employment agency.

VIP International
VIP House, 17 Charing Cross Road, London WC2H 0EP. Tel: (0171) 930 0541.

An employment agency which can place mainly Hotel, Catering and Bar Department staff. Not all vacancies handled are on ships.

Windstar Cruises
300 Elliott Avenue West, Seattle, Washington State, WA98119, USA. Tel: 206 281 3535.

Windstar is a sail cruise line operating three sail cruise ships.

World Explorer Cruises
555 Montgomery Street, San Francisco, CA94111, USA. Tel: 415 393 1565.

This cruise line's single ship operates as a floating department of the University of Pittsburgh during the winter and offers cruises to Alaska in the summer. As such it has different crew requirements from a regular line.

Zerbone Cruise Ship Services
Suite 700, 100 South Biscayne Boulevard, Miami, FL33131, USA.

Employment agency for Catering and Bar Department crew.

FERRY COMPANIES

Brittany Ferries, Millbay Docks, Plymouth PL1 3EW. Tel: (01752) 221321.

Caledonian McBrayne Ltd, Ferry Terminal, Gourock, Renfrewshire PA19 1QP. Tel: (01475) 33755.

P&O North Sea Ferries, King George V Dock, Hedon Road, Hull HU9 5QA. Tel: (01482) 795141.

Irish Ferries, Alexandra Road, Dublin, Eire. Tel: 0001 788077.

P&O European Ferries, Channel House, Channel View Road, Dover CT17 9TJ. Tel: (01304) 22300.

Sally Line, Argyle Centre, York Street, Ramsgate, Kent CT11 9PL. Tel: (01843) 595566.

Sealink Scotland, 4 – 6 South Strand Street, Stranraer DG9 7JW.

Stena Line, PO Box 31300, S40519 Gothenburg, Sweden.

Stena Sealink Ltd, Charger House, PO Box 121, Park Street, Ashford, Kent TN24 8EX. Tel: (01233) 647022.

Other Useful Addresses

PROFESSIONAL AND TRADE ORGANISATIONS

Academy of Wine Service, Five Kings House, 1 Queen Street Place, London EC4R 1QS. Tel: (01483) 302373.

Association of Marine Catering and Supply, 30/32 St Mary Axe, London EC3A 8ET.

Chamber of Shipping, Merchant Navy Training Board, Carthusian Court, Carthusian Street, London EC1M 6EB. Tel: (0171) 417 8400.

Construction Industry Training Board (CITB), Bircham Newton Training Centre, Bircham Newton, King's Lynn, Norfolk PE31 6RH. Tel: (01553) 776677.

Court of Master Sommeliers, 27 St Matthews Road, Chelston, Torquay, Devon TQ2 6JA. Tel: (01803) 605031.

EURES, Overseas Placing Unit, Level 4, Skills House, 3 – 7 Holy Green, Sheffield S1 4AQ. Tel: (0114) 259 6051.

General Council of British Shipping, 30 – 32 St Mary Axe, London EC3A 8ET. Tel: (0171) 283 2922.

Hotel and Catering Training Company, International House, High Street, Ealing, London W5 5DB. Tel: (0181) 579 2400.

Hotel, Catering & Institutional Management Association (HCIMA), 191 Trinity Road, London SW17 7HN. Tel: (0181) 672 4251.

Merchant Navy Training School, Warsash Maritime Centre, Southampton Institute, Newtown Road, Warsash, Southampton SO3 9ZL. Tel: (01489) 576161.

National Council for Vocational Qualifications, 222 Euston Road, London NW1 2BZ. Tel: (0171) 387 9898.

National Sea Training College, Denton, Gravesend, Kent DA12 2HR. Tel: (01474) 363656.

National Union of Rail, Maritime and Transport Workers (RMT), Unity House, Euston Road, London NW1 2BL. Tel: (0171) 387 4771.

Port of Miami Authority, 1001 North America Way, Miami, FL33152, USA.

Seafarers Indefatigable School, Plas Llanfair, Llanfairpwll, Anglesey LL61 6NT. Tel: (01248) 714338.

Ship Safe Training Group Ltd, 2nd Floor, 135 High Street, Rochester, Kent ME1 1EW. Tel: (01634) 405252.

United Kingdom Bartenders Guild, 91–93 Gordon Road, Harborne, Birmingham B17 9HA. Tel: (0121) 427 8099.

Wine & Spirit Education Trust (WSET), Five Kings House, 1 Queen Street Place, London EC4R 1QS. Tel: (0171) 236 3551.

BOOKS

Berlitz Complete Guide to Cruising and Cruise Ships, Douglas Ward (Berlitz Publishing Company).

Crews for Cruise, John Kenning (Harp Publications).

Fodor's Cruises and Ports of Call (Fodor's Travel Publications Inc).

Frommer's Cruises, Marylyn Springer (Macmillan Travel).

How to Get a Job in Hotels & Catering, Mark Hempshell (How To Books).

How to Get a Job in Travel & Tourism, Mark Hempshell (How To Books).

How to Master Languages, Roger Jones (How To Books).

Lloyd's Register of Ships (Lloyd's Register of Shipping).

The Handbook of Tourism, English Tourist Board (Hobsons Publishing plc).

Working as a Holiday Rep, Steve Marks (How To Books).

NEWSPAPERS, TRADE JOURNALS AND NEWSLETTERS

Caterer and Hotelkeeper, Quadrant House, The Quadrant, Sutton, Surrey SM2 5AS. Tel: (0181) 652 3500.

Catering Update and Caterer and Hotelkeeper Helpline (an enquiry and information service aiming to answer questions on the hotel and catering trade). Tel: (0839) 373737.

Innovative Cruise Services, 36 Midlothian Drive, Glasgow G41 3QU. Tel: (0141) 649 8644 (publishes a quarterly vacancy bulletin).

Jobs International, Magmaker Ltd, Cromwell Court, New Road, St Ives, Cambridgeshire PE17 4BG.

K L Smith's Cruise Letter, Lane Publishing, PO Box 761, Virgil, Ontario, Canada LO5 1TO. e-mail: ksmith@lane.on.ca

Overseas Jobs Express, Premier House, Shoreham Airport, Sussex BN43 5FF. Tel: (01273) 440220.

The Stage and Television Today, 47 Bermondsey Street, London SE1 3XT. Tel: (0171) 403 1818.

Travel Trade Gazette, Morgan Grampian House, Calderwood Street, London SE18 6QH. Tel: (0181) 855 7777.

Travel Weekly, Quadrant House, The Quadrant, Sutton, Surrey SM2 5AS. Tel: (0181) 652 3799.

Glossary of Technical Terms

Abeam. Off the side of the ship, at a right angle to its length.

Aft. Near, toward or in the rear of the ship.

Alleyway. A passageway or corridor.

Amidships. In or toward the middle of the ship; the longitudinal centre portion of the ship.

Astern. At or toward the stern (back) of the ship.

Backwash. Motion in the water caused by the propeller(s) moving in a reverse (astern) direction.

Bar. Sandbar, usually caused by tidal or current conditions near the shore.

Beam. Width of the ship between its two sides at the widest point.

Bearing. Compass direction, expressed in degrees, from the ship to a particular objective or destination.

Berth. Dock, pier or quay. Also means bed on board ship.

Bilge. Lowermost spaces of the infrastructure of a ship.

Bow. The forwardmost part of the vessel.

Bridge. Navigational and command control centre.

Bulkhead. Upright partition (wall) dividing the ship into compartments.

Companionway. Interior stairway.

Course. Direction in which the ship is headed, in degrees.

Davit. A device for raising and lowering lifeboats.

Deadlight. A ventilated porthole cover to prevent light from entering.

Deck. Berth, pier or quay.

Draft (or draught). Measurement in feet from the ship's waterline to the lowest point of its keel.

Fantail. The rear or overhang of the ship.

Fathom. Measurement of distance equal to six feet.

Free port. Port or place that is free of customs duty and regulations.

Funnel. Chimney from which the ship's combustion gases are propelled into the atmosphere.

Galley. The ship's kitchen.

Gangplank/gangway. The stairway or ramp link between ship and shore.

Gross registered ton (grt). A measurement of 100 cubic feet of enclosed revenue earning space within a vessel. This is the standard system of measuring passenger ships used for classification by the Lloyds Register, the British ship surveying society.

Helm. This is the machinery which steers the ship.

House flag. This flag identifies the line to which a particular ship belongs.

Hull. The main 'body' of the ship, not including the superstructure.

Leeward. The side which is away from the wind.

Manifest. A listing of all the ship's passengers and crew.

Pitch. The rise and fall of the ship's bow, which happens when the ship is under way in a heavy sea.

Port. The left side of a ship when facing forward.

Quay. Dock, berth, pier.

Rudder. A fin-like device at the stern and below the water, which steers the ship.

Screw. The ship's propeller.

Smokestack. The funnel.

Stabiliser. A gyroscopically operated fin which extends from either/both side(s) of a ship, below the water, and which creates extra stability.

Starboard. The right side of the ship when facing forward.

Stern. The back of the ship, furthest away from the bow.

Tender. A smaller vessel, often a lifeboat, used to transport passengers between the ship and shore when the vessel is at anchor.

Wake. The track of agitated water left behind a ship when in motion.

Waterline. The line along the side of a ship's hull corresponding to the surface of the water.

Windward. The side toward which the wind blows.

Yaw. The erratic deviation from the ship's set course, usually caused by a heavy sea.

Index